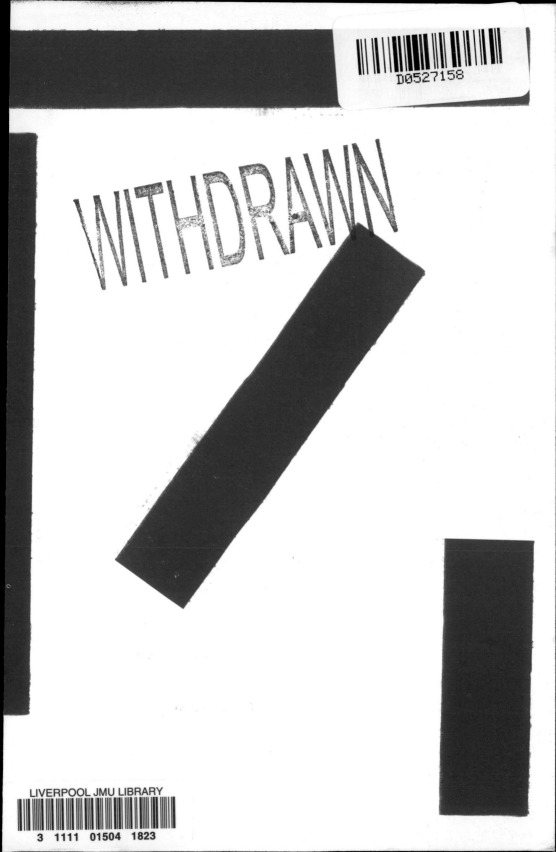

JOINED FORCES
AUDIENCE PARTICIPATION IN THEATRE

EDITED BY
ANNA R. BURZYŃSKA

A publication by **House on Fire**

House on Fire is supported by the **Culture Programme of the European Union.**

The European Commission support for the production
of this publication does not constitute an endorsement
of the contents which reflects the views only of the authors,
and the Commission cannot be held responsible for any use
which may be made of the information contained therein.

Culture

House on Fire are:
Archa Theatre (Prague), BIT Teatergarasjen (Bergen), brut Wien (Vienna), Frascati Theater (Amsterdam),
HAU Hebbel am Ufer (Berlin), Kaaitheater (Brussels), LIFT (London), Malta Festival Poznań,
Maria Matos Teatro Municipal / EGEAC (Lisbon) and Théâtre Garonne (Toulouse).

JOINED FORCES

AUDIENCE PARTICIPATION IN THEATRE

EDITED BY
ANNA R. BURZYŃSKA

JOINED FORCES
AUDIENCE PARTICIPATION IN THEATRE

PERFORMING URGENCY #3

Edited by
Anna R. Burzyńska

Performing Urgency Series Editor:
Florian Malzacher

Graphic Design:
R2

Copy Editing:
Harriet Curtis

Editorial Management:
Laura Lopes

Translations:
John Barrett (48), Jane Bemont (134), Leonilda Saraiva dos Anjos (62, 88, 98, 120), Peter Welchman (76)

Photos:
Adelheid|Female Economy (165, 166), Pamela Albarracín (93), David Baltzer (78, 81, 184, 185), Julia Bauer (53), Blenda (94), Kristien Van den Brande (64), Richard Duyck (67), Zuzanna Głowacka (37, 40, 45, 46), InCompany (56), Kamerich & Budwilowitz (160), Sjoerd Knibbeler (161), Daniel Koch (82), Gunnar Lusch (55), Luca Mattei (57), Opavivará! (101, 102), Rimini Protokoll (128, 129), TeatroValleOccupato (21), Benno Tobler (125), Tea Tupajić (141, 142, 144, 145, 146, 147, 148), Antonio Vuković (151)

Publisher:
**Alexander
Verlag Berlin**
Fredericiastraße 8
D-14050 Berlin

Co-publisher:
Live Art Development Agency
The White Building
Unit 7, Queen's Yard
White Post Lane, London E9 5EN

Printed in Maia (Portugal) by Maiadouro
ISBN 978-3-89581-427-3
Legal Deposit 417855/16

ANTI-MANIFESTOS

EXPERIENCES

The nineteenth century was a century of actors. The twentieth century was a century of directors. The twenty-first century is a century of spectators. With Jacques Rancière's *The Emancipated Spectator* (2009) being the most discussed theatre-related text of the last decade, there is an increase in scholarly and curatorial interest in the most mysterious, potentially dangerous and, in fact, most important participant of the performance, who stays silent, motionless, and hidden in darkness: the audience. And similarly, artists desire to finally 'meet the spectators': to let them speak, get into a dialogue with them, invite them to involve themselves in pursuing the performance. To liberate the audience.

There are many different factors that contribute to this unexpected turn. Probably the most important one is the importance of political theatre today: artists engage in contemporary social and political issues, and scholars highlight performative aspects of political life and political aspects of theatre performances. In the world where democracy, activism, and freedom of speech become more and more important (and more and more endangered) values, theatre shouldn't be a place where one is supposed to remain passive and silent and to accept everything that is said. Just the opposite: theatre has the potential to become a kind of 'rehearsal space' for democracy, a place where one's encouraged not only to observe, but to be critical, active, and responsible for what is happening (like in Bertolt Brecht's 'Lehrstücke' ('Learning Plays') and in Augusto Boal's idea of 'spect-actors'). Instead of traditional theatre that focused on the idea of passive people whose fate and destiny was decided by the gods (like puppets on strings controlled from above by artists), the contemporary world demands a different model: showing people that fate and destiny is their hands and they can change the plot of their lives (and change the world) in each moment. Just as they can change the shape of performances participating in them.

But there are other important factors as well. One of them is how new media have changed the way information is received – in interactive, selective, and dialogical ways. The gap between 'old-fashioned' spectators sitting in front of the radio or television and today's video game players and internet users is huge – new consumers of information and entertainment literally take matters into their own hands, choosing preferred content, navigating the story in non-linear, network style, commenting, and adding their own content.

There's also been a significant shift in theory that has put the audience into the spotlight. Performance studies stretched the meaning behind the word 'performance' far beyond traditional theatre with stage and audience, incorporating ideas of contemporary anthropology, sociology, and philosophy of language into theatre studies, proving that in our everyday life we are all performers and spectators – at the same time. Also postdramatic theatre – as described by Hans-Thies Lehmann (2006) – very often requires the spectators to become active co-writers of the performance.

For a very long time, one of the most powerful weapons of political theatre (from *fin-de-siècle* cabaret through Dadaists, Futurists, and Bertolt Brecht to Christoph Schlingensief) was offending the audience (to quote the title of the Peter Handke's play from 1966). Revolted, left-wing artists tried to provoke conservative middle class audiences in the principle of '*épater le bourgeois*'. Now strategies are different: more and more, artists try to invite members of the audience – especially those who are for some reason (economic, racial, cultural, religious, gender, language, etc.) excluded from society, have no political power and no chance to make their voices heard – to make theatre together. Art becomes much more powerful when performers and spectators join forces. Hence the title of this book.

Joined Forces: Audience Participation in Theatre presents various examples of audience participation in theatre linking them to problems of participation in democracy and to socially engaged art. Making theatre is always a political statement – asking about audience participation practices is asking about the possibilities of making changes both in art and in politics.

The book opens with three introductory texts that serve as the theoretical foundation for the rest of the publication. Jan

Sowa reflects upon political modes of participation, analysing how the notions of 'the public' and 'the common' change in the era of Occupy movement. Dominique Nduhura diagnoses the uneasy and ever changing relationship between forum theatre and politics in the African context, and Antoine Pickels examines the current revival of participatory art forms in Europe as a big opportunity and a big risk at the same time, since making participation 'fashionable' leads to destroying the very sense of the idea.

The core part of the book consist of 11 essays and interviews. Artists from different countries were asked to reflect on the idea of participation, to share their experiences and write about their successes and failures, hopes and doubts. While it's impossible to create a map of participatory art, choosing (nearly) a dozen various representative and remarkable examples can help to outline the situation of contemporary political, audience-engaging theatre as seen by its creators themselves.

The first two texts focus on places: institutions that became meeting points and enabled potential spectators, who had previously been excluded, not only to watch performances but to actively participate in them. Justine Boutens introduces a group of different artists working at the Flemish CAMPO art centre in Ghent, and Miriam Tscholl in conversation with Elena Basteri presents Bürgerbühne in Dresden as a place that enables direct communication between 'punks, bankers, followers of Judaism and Islam, midwives, undertakers, fans of the Dynamo Dresden football team and men in the midst of a midlife crisis'.

The next part of the book is entitled 'Anti-manifestos', as it challenges apparent dichotomies between a mechanism of participation as a promise of emancipation and a traditional mechanism as a guarantee of oppression (Roger Bernat and Roberto Fratini Serafide), individual and collective (Ophélia Patrício Arrabal), political and aesthetic (Ana Vujanović). The authors balance artistic, curatorial, and academic point of views, setting together different theories, notions, and ideas and calling the 'participatory utopia' into question.

The final six contributions describe artists' experiences, including successful and failed attempts to invite the audience to co-create theatre. Tobi Müller interviews Rimini Protokoll members (Helgard Haug, Stefan Kaegi, and Daniel Wetzel) whose idea of replacing professional actors with 'experts of the everyday' has become emblematic for contemporary documentary theatre. Lotte van den Berg writes about her long-term project *Building*

Conversation, that examines conversation 'as a joint creation, a collective improvisation, a work of art'. Tea Tupajić recalls her work in Israel and events that inspired the creation of a performative installation *The Disco*. Adelheid Roosen speaks to Tom Sellar about projects created via her foundation Adelheid|Female Economy that challenge the new ethos of intercultural exchange. Wojtek Ziemilski makes a list of different problems with participation that he has encountered when trying to activate his audience and create a common space for both artists and spectators. Finally, Johanna Freiburg and Bastian Trost from Gob Squad in conversation with Adam Czirak discuss different strategies of involving not only theatre-goers, but also passers-by into their performances.

Of course, the book lacks many important names: from 'founding fathers' (and mothers) like Augusto Boal, Guillermo Gómez-Peña, and members of the Living Theatre through Jeremy Deller, inviting huge masses of people to take part in his reenactments of historical events, to diverse young artists such as duo deufert&plischke, experimenting with participative choreography, and Laila Soliman, whose performances are genuine 'lessons of revolting' for spectators in Arab countries. Some of these artists already appeared in *Not Just a Mirror: Looking for the Political Theatre of Today* and *Turn, Turtle! Reenacting the Institute*, the first and the second part of the publication series Performing Urgency; the list of important politically involved theatre artists around the world, whose work deserves analysis, could go on and on. I hope that the end of this book will be a beginning of another.

Anna R. Burzyńska

JAN SOWA

IT'S POLITICAL ECONOMY, STUPID!

TOWARDS PROGRESSIVE MODES OF PARTICIPATION

14

Crisis, or a moment of judgement

The feeling of crisis and exhaustion of the mainstream politics has become widespread in contemporary societies and as such it cuts across the spectrum of social positions and ideological worldviews. Patterns of socio-political life deeply entrenched in many societies in the postwar period are eroding among a popular conviction that the politicians of various levels – from local to international – elected to represent us and to govern in our interest fail to enact this obligation in their everyday decisions.

Symptoms of this exhaustion take various forms. The most visible one is the career of the so called anti-establishment candidates and parties that successfully challenge well established figures and formations of mainstream politics. It is happening all over the world from the United States to the Philippines, to Austria, to Spain, to Poland. Other symptoms include calls for restitution of monarchy, conservative attempts to save the remains of the past from ubiquitous and accelerating transformations, right-wing populisms successfully conquering the votes of those who fall victim to the *status quo* yet do not have enough social and cultural capital to opt for a more progressive solution and – last but not least – actions of individuals and groups striving for more participation as a solution to the chronic political crisis we have found ourselves in. These progressive demands prove that we are also facing an opportunity. The word 'crisis' derives from Greek κρίσις, meaning also 'a turning point' and 'a moment of judgement'. Any future turn of events depends ultimately on our ability to properly judge the situation we are in.

Paradoxically enough, the demands for more participative social and political arrangements come from two fundamentally opposing political positions and for this reason they convey a radically different message, even if they use the same words such as 'citizen', 'bottom-up', 'civic activity', 'autonomy', 'initiative', etc. On the one hand participation is a buzzword for the liberal centre and, in this tradition, it is best articulated by the concept of 'civil society' (as explored by such authors as Seymour Martin Lipset in his book *Political Man*, 1960, or Robert D. Putnam in *Making Democracy Work*, 1993). On the other, inclusion and participation occupy a central position in the leftwing rhetoric and epitomise a broader project of 'radical' or 'real democracy'. Even if these terms may refer to various practical solutions (for example, see C. Douglas Lummis, *Radical Democracy*, 1997; David Trend (ed.), *Radical Democracy: Identity, Citizenship, and the State*, 1996; and Michael Hardt and Antonio Negri, 'The Fight for "Real Democracy" at the Heart of Occupy Wall Street', in *Foreign Affairs*, 2011), its main goal boils down to reinvigoration of ailing democratic institutions by encouraging and enabling people to take part in a more open political process. This complex and in many ways paradoxical theoretical and ideological landscape is mirrored closely in rhizomatic nature of global social and political struggle as it was revealed by the events of 2011 in Middle East, Northern Africa, Europe, and the United States. It was the year that can justly be called 'the year of the people' as it was marked by intense and widespread mobilisation against the powers that be and ubiquitous calls for more participation in political decision making. Its synchronization within a space of a dozen months should come as no surprise. We are dealing here with a global cycle of struggles starting with anti-globalisation protest in 1999 in Seattle, developing through opposition to wars in Iraq and Afghanistan, amplified by failures of mainstream political, social, and economic institutions revealed by the financial crisis of 2008, and culminating in the formidable 'year of dreaming dangerously' – as Slavoj Žižek in *The Year of Dreaming Dangerously* (2013) called this period – in 2011.

The link between the movements in the Middle East/North Africa and Europe/United States has been underlined and expressed by activists, such as Anna Curcio and Gigi Roggero, or a multitude of occupiers on Liberty Plaza in New York on many occasions (see Curcio and Roggero: 'Tunisia is our University – Notes and Reflections from the Liberation Without Borders Tour', in *University in Crisis*, 2011; and 'Protests of 2011 Timeline', in *The Occupied Wall*

Street Journal, 2011). However, putting various events of the year 2011 in a unified conceptual frame may seem a little bit far-fetched, to put it mildly. We can very well understand why, for example, people in Egypt or Tunisia were fighting for democracy – in other words, for a bigger participation in political life. They were citizens of brutal dictatorships deprived of liberties typical for western democracies, especially of the right to take part in unbiased electoral process. But how is it possible that citizens of democratic states were fighting for democracy? After all, the protests erupted within the European Union and the United States – political formations believed to be democratic and thus allowing for their citizens to participate in political process in various forms: voting, engaging in election campaigns, running for office, petitioning media, taking concerns to court, etc. The democratic Western regimes seem to be built on the idea of political inclusion and participation, so how can one 'fight for democracy' there when it does not come to pathologies such as corruption or stolen elections? This widespread political commonsense clearly coincides with the equally common conviction that political systems in the West have become alienated, do not allow for proper participation, and thus should be regarded as un-democratic. In order to make something out of this confusion we need to briefly trace back in time development of Western parliamentary regime. It will also allow us to articulate the difference between the liberal and progressive modes of participation, casting more light on the contemporary social, political, and ideological landscape surrounding the ideas and practices of participation.

Democracy versus parliamentarism, or two modes of participation

Popular convictions and linguistic usus tend to equate parliamentarism with democracy. This confusion goes sometimes as far as identification of parliamentarism with the 'rule of the people' as the very term 'demo-cracy' conveys. As a matter of fact the latter existed in Ancient Greece and had little to do with contemporary democratic regimes. Not only because the large part of the Greek demos was excluded from any participation in political power – mostly women, slaves, and 'foreign residents' or μέτοικοι – but mainly due to a very particular and singular organisation of political life. Ancient Greeks did not vote. They exercised a combination of direct democracy – mass rallies – and administrative rule, however the members of administration were not voted in, they were chosen by lot. For this reason contemporary attempts to put our political institutions

17

in line with Greek inspirations – such as, for example, the idea of 'demarchy', put forward by Australian philosopher John Burnheim (cited in Brian Martin, 'Demarchy: A Democratic Alternative to Electoral Politics', 1992) – sometimes go under a wholesale label of 'lottocracy' (see Alexander Guerro, 'The Lottocracy', 2014). Contrary to contemporary notions of what democracy is, the Ancient Greeks did not consider election process to be the best embodiment of the idea of equal participation in power. It looks like they were very aware of the same dangers that devour contemporary parliamentary regimes. They wanted to get rid of demagogy – which literary means 'a leadership of the mob' – by which outspoken and cunning individuals exercise power via rhetorical means over uneducated masses, making them act in the interest of the demagogue and thus fatally influencing any electoral process (we do not need to look far to see what they dreaded: Donald Trump). They were aware that rich, intelligent, and good-looking people have a much better chance of succeeding in elections than the poor, uneducated, and ugly – due to, precisely, their wealth (i.e. resources and influence), knowledge (tools to manipulate the masses), and physical appeal (see John Dunn (ed.), *Democracy: The Unfinished Journey 508 BC to AD 1993*, 1993). What's more, the election process opens up a career path for the most power hungry individuals and the Ancient Greeks believed, as Jacques Rancière points out in his book *On the Shores of Politics* (2007), that the most eager to rule should not be allowed to hold power as they are the ones who become tyrants. Choosing the rulers by lot eliminated all these dangers and allowed for construction of a government more representative of people's opinions and ideas. We can right away grasp what the Greeks meant if we refer to the methodology of contemporary social research (in academia or in opinion polls): the most representative research sample is the one randomly composed.

It would be difficult to find procedural resemblances between the ancient and modern democracies. They are mainly connected by the word 'democracy' used to describe both of them and by a general conviction that people should take part in exercising power. Besides this very vague similarity we live in a very different system. Its essence lies not in 'government of the people' but in balancing the influence of various social agents – individuals, classes, organisations, status groups, etc. – and as such it stems from the feudal practice of consultation between the king and the nobles that evolved into liberal representative institutions known as national parliaments. The founding document of contemporary democracy did not originate in ancient Greece or Rome but in Northern Europe – it is the Magna Carta from 1215, a testimony of a compromise between the king and aristocratic class.

Exploring the genealogy of parliamentarism goes far beyond the scope of this text. However, one detail needs to be underlined: the mechanism of parliamentary representation through universal suffrage was devised as a compromise between the emerging political subjectivity of the people and elites' eagerness to keep it under control. It is clearly visible in discussions that led to the establishment of the first fully functioning parliamentary regime – the United States of America. Its founding fathers made a definite distinction between democracy and republic, deliberately distancing themselves from the former and aiming at the latter. Democracy was the rule of the people, republic – rule of their representatives. Alexander Hamilton and James Madison were particularly clear about it (see Hamilton, 'The Union as a Safeguard Against Domestic Faction and Insurrection', 1787; Madison, 'The Same Subject Continued', 1787, and 'The Senate Continued', 1788). As Madison suggests, what characterised the American representative government was 'the total exclusion of the people, in their collective capacity, from any share in the latter [i.e. in the government]'. This is the reason why the US Constitution does not envision a possibility of conducting a federal referendum as it is a form of popular power in its 'collective capacity', while on the federal level, power resides solely in the hands of the representatives, thus people do not participate directly in power.

To complete this image we have to ponder for a moment upon the voting process itself. Isn't it the very mechanism of participation, of expressing our will and of directly shaping the government? We have, after all, also passive voting rights, which means that technically any and each of us can be elected to any position. There are several problems here that help to explain why the demands and ideas of participation are so appealing to critics of Western democracies.

Let's start with the question of general eligibility to run in elections. This is precisely where we seem to be much dumber than the Ancients: guarantee of equal passive suffrage – right to be elected – for everyone is an empty formal rule never fulfilled in any actual existing society. If we want a genuine and general participation in power as the factual outcome of the political process and not just a formal presupposition devoid of any meaning, electing representatives is not the way to go. It is rather an opportunity for

19

the rich, the good-looking, and the outspoken to obtain unproportioned share in power. Theoretically every citizen can become a president or a prime minister, however the situation is very different in practical terms. Money translates into more impact in the media and more outreach in direct campaigning. Cultural and social capital also matter and it is not an accident that an important part of British political establishment comes from Eaton and many French politicians, regardless of their political convictions, graduated from École nationale d'administration.

There are pertinent sociological and politological theories that grasp this anti-democratic element of parliamentary regimes. Joseph Schumpeter in his book *Capitalism, Socialism, and Democracy* (2008) coined the term 'competitive leadership', suggesting that the election process allows citizens not to rule but to decide which contesting candidate they want to be ruled by. Parliamentary government is not an expression of people's will or sovereignty, but of their consent. It is a major difference that we understand right away when it is put in these terms: actively willing something is very different from just passively agreeing on something to happen. The latter is very far from participation and it is precisely this feature of parliamentarism that creates a feeling of alienation – the opposite of participation – so widespread among citizens of contemporary democracy.

American political scientist Robert Dahl suggested, in his book *Polyarchy: Participation and Opposition* (1971), a better name for what we call democracy: a polyarchy. 'Poly' stands for 'many' and 'archy' for loci of power – parliamentarism is a combination of many heterodox forms of power. It has got a democratic component, but also an oligarchic one (for example the influence of money on politics) and aristocratic one (unproportioned influence of social elites). As a result, only a fraction of actual power lies in the hands of popular sovereign. Citizens of a parliamentary state participate in power, but only to a limited degree, as they have to share it with other undemocratic groups and institutions; not what we have in mind when we talk about parliamentarism as 'sovereignty of the people'.

This slightly long historical account has been necessary as it allows us to articulate the basic difference between liberal and radical (or progressive) ideas of participation as well as the clash between them. I deliberately do not use the terms 'right' and 'left'. Despite its intense criticism I believe they remain useful to some extent, especially if understood in Hegelian terms as different

The Occupation of Teatro Valle (Rome), 18 April 2012

approaches to the relation between reality and rationality (boiling down to question: 'Does reality have to adjust to rationality, as the left believes, or vice versa as holds the right in conservative or liberal versions?'). However, in the present context I find it more convenient to use a different set of terms: 'conservative', 'liberal', and 'progressive/radical' to describe what is called, respectively, 'the right', 'the centre', and 'the left' of the political spectrum.

The liberals see participation as a complimentary mechanism, useful in carrying out those collective tasks that are best managed by local community of citizens. Participation is not seen as alternative to political representation but as a part of socio-political mix, where representation and participation belong to two distinct spheres: the ones of political society and the civil society, respectively. Contrary to this view the progressive ideology defines participation as a way of at least reforming the mechanisms of power – i.e. of political society – and at best of getting rid of them altogether in their present form while replacing them with more participatory and thus less alienating arrangements. Let's take a brief look at these two modes or concepts of participation.

The uses and abuses of civil society

The liberal reflection on participation and bottom-up activities has got quite a long tradition and has been developed mostly by the scholars, thinkers and researchers within the Anglo-American tradition. As a matter of fact, it was a journey undertaken by a European to the United States in the early nineteenth century that gave birth to this current of reflection and investigation. For it was precisely people's eagerness to participate in civic activities via various kinds of associations that fascinated the French aristocrat, Alexis de Tocqueville during his trip to America. As he wrote in his opus magnum, *Democracy in America* (1835):

> Americans of all ages, all conditions, all minds constantly unite. Not only do they have commercial and industrial associations in which *all take part* [emphasis added], but they also have a thousand other kinds: religious, moral, grave, futile, very general and very particular, immense and very small; Americans use associations to give fêtes, to found seminaries, to build inns, to raise churches, to distribute books, to send missionaries to the antipodes; in this manner they create hospitals, prisons, schools. [...] Everywhere that, at the head of a new undertaking, you see the government in France and a great lord in England, count on it that you will perceive an association in the United States.

Tocqueville's fascination with this enormous citizens' participation and its importance for general society found its continuation in widespread research on what came to be known as social capital and associate with interpersonal trust, one of the key concepts of contemporary social theory. It was mainly American anthropologist, Edward Banfield, whose research on underdevelopment conducted in Southern Italy in the 1950s (see Edward C. Banfield, *Moral Basis of a Backward Society*, 1958) paved the way for making willingness to participate, associate, and cooperate one of the key research topics in twentieth-century sociology. The single most important investigation into the significance of citizens' bottom-up grassroots participation was also undertaken in Italy in the 1970s by American sociologist Robert D. Putnam and presented in the above-mentioned book *Making Democracy Work: Civic Traditions in Modern Italy* (1993). This meticulous research provided the empirical proof that the level of civic participation as mirrored by the number of NGOs in a given region correlates very closely with various indicators of social, political, and economic growth. The places, where people participate in common tasks are better organised, wealthier, and have happier populations than the regions where the level of participation is low (see Pierre Bourdieu, 'The Forms of Capital', 1986; James S. Coleman, 'Social Capital in the Creation of Human Capital', 1988; Jane Jacobs, *The Death and Life of Great American Cities*, 1961; and Robert D. Putnam, *Bowling Alone: The Collapse and Revival of American Community*, 2000).

Progressive participation

Although there should be no doubt that participation, trust, and social capital make societies work better, there's also a series of limitations and problems linked with this tradition of thought and activism. The oldest and the most important line of criticism goes all the way back to Marx and to his attack on Hegel's concept of civil society as such (Karl Marx, *Critique of Hegel's Philosophy Of Right*, 1844). The basic flaw that Marx saw there was a complete lack of interest in the questions of political economy. The notion of 'civil society' creates a vision of formal equality among citizens and of their agency that remains an illusion, because it does not take into account asymmetries of wealth and status among various social classes. It is reflected in a complete lack of interest in the question of property and of means of production and redistribution among the advocates of civil society. Marx and his followers believed that a huge part of the problems within modern capitalist societies stems precisely from the unjust distribution of fruits of labour among various agents participating in the production process. Despite liberal claims of empowerment of individuals, citizens have no say over the property relations within capitalist society, while the entire concept of civic participation serves to manage problems created by this predicament. To put it in concrete and up-to-date terms with an example, the bourgeois strategy would be, for instance, to organise cities in ways best suited for capital owners – car makers, developers, real-estate agencies, etc. – leaving citizens with an option to self-organise in a participatory way to deal with the fallout of such policies such as air pollution, rent hikes, foreclosures, evictions, conversion of green areas into parking lots, etc. Any solution that the civil society comes up with has to be in line with the most sacred element of the bourgeois order: the private property; progressive and radical solutions – like, for example, abandoning private property of land within cities in order to better manage collective interests of their dwellers – are not on the table. Participation stops at the door of property.

Another, more practical problem, is a wide rift separating the liberal idea of citizens' participation from its contemporary practice. It is epitomised in the fate of the NGO model that has suffered a fundamental distortion. Buzzwords such as 'citizens' participation' or 'grassroots activity' serve as an excuse for the government to shift a huge chunk of its duties and responsibilities to the shoulders of civil society. The process has been researched in detail in the United States and elsewhere (see Steven Rathgeb Smith and Michael Lipsky, *Nonprofits for Hire: The Welfare State in the Age of Contracting,* 1993; and Agnieszka Rymsza, 'Partnerzy służby publicznej? Wyzwania współpracy sektora pozarządowego z administracją publiczną w świetle doświadczeń amerykańskich', 2005). It boils down to making civic organisations dependent on state and regional authorities via a system of grants. It turns NGOs into de facto para-companies, a sort of government contractor receiving money to work along priorities they have no part in shaping. This negative development is called 'governamentalisation' of the third sector and has been mocked by the invention of the term GONGO: a Government Organised Nongovernmental Organisation. The supposed autonomy of civil society turns out to be a fiction. Civil society has become, as a matter of fact, a part of political society disguised in participative slogans.

The progressive take on participation stems from different assessments, aims at different goals and uses different strategies. Firstly and most often, the progressive idea of participation does not treat participation as a mechanism complimentary to political representation, but as a major game changer in the political game as such. From this perspective the very institution of parliamentary representation is regarded as the main enemy of participation. It needs to be underlined that the progressive tradition looks at the history of representative institution in a different way than the liberal one. For the liberals, parliamentarism is mainly a result of compromise between the old aristocratic elite and the new social hegemon, the bourgeoisie, and was developed in the interests of general society as a universal conflict solving tool (see Norberto Bobbio, *Liberalism and Democracy,* 1990). The progressives point to the fact that there was a third party in this bargain – the people. The interests and goals of the popular classes were in conflict with both the aristocracy and bourgeoisie. The liberals believed that the conservative attitude towards the masses was impractical and would lead to some sort of popular revolution that would turn the world upside-down destroying all property relations. On the other hand, the popular hatred towards aristocracy was a force acting in favour of the bourgeoisie and was used on many occasions to further the own goals of the new propertied classes against the old ones. Parliamentarism seemed a perfect tool to empower popular classes in such a way as to keep them safe for the bourgeoisie: by incorporating them in the process of constituting power in such a manner as not to let them actually participate in the everyday functioning of government, as it was deliberately put by Madison in the passage quoted above (see Immanuel Wallerstein, *The Agonies of Liberalism: What Hope Progress?*, 1994). For the progressive radicals participation is not an idea and practice that should ameliorate the liberal institutions by complementing them, but a revolutionary postulate aiming at fundamental transformation of societies. For this reason the progressive vindications of the right to participate go further than the liberal ones, both in theory and in practice.

Firstly, the progressive tradition demands participation in the actual, everyday functioning of political institution. To put it in precise philosophical terms, the progressives do not accept the fact that the constituent power of the people is realised uniquely in the act of establishing a constituted power. This distinction goes back to the philosophy of Baruch Spinoza. Though there is no place to explore it in detail here, it has been formidably analysed by others on various occasions (see Antonio Negri, *Insurgencies: Constituent Power and the Modern State,* 1998; and Paolo Virno, *A Grammar of the Multitude: For an Analysis of Contemporary Forms of Life,* 2004). The most important fact that stems from this revolt is the questioning of the liberal idea of parliamentary representation, where the representative is not bound by its constituency's opinions or instructions (he or she can vote as they please) and cannot be recalled from office before their mandate expires at the end of each electoral turn.

As a result of all above-mentioned problems, the progressive advocates of political participation would like to see parliamentarism abolished, but they want it to happen in an emancipatory way, giving place to more democratic forms of organising political power. It's an attempt to democratise polyarchy – to use Dalh's terms – by enhancing its democratic element via means of participation and diminishing the role of undemocratic elements such as status, wealth, etc. It does not mean a direct, rally democracy. Representation is not rejected but reformed along more controllable lines – representatives ought to be guided and limited by instructions from their constituencies to take certain positions, they can be recalled for mandatory consultations by those who elected them and their mandate can be revoked by those who entrusted the given representative with it if he or she does not act according to terms agreed.

This way of participating in power via representatives is different from direct democracy. According to its proponents this more participative and more democratic solution would allow the curbing of several major malaises of parliamentarism: the damaging influence of money in politics, the problem of lobbying, and the pest of broken campaign promises. The politicians would not be able to say whatever pleases their constituencies during campaigns and then do whatever they find personally suitable for reasons they do need to disclose. Representatives would be elected to enact their promises and could be deprived of their mandate by those who trusted them if they fail to act along these promises.

The second most important distinction between liberal and progressive view of participation goes back to the question of political economy put forward by Marx more than 150 years ago. Liberal democracy seems to be enacting the notion of popular control over social life, however, it leaves one zone completely outside of any democratic control: the economy. On the general level we have no say in setting the goals of economic activities that remain ruled by the market mechanisms (constructed, to be sure, by states, so by collective agents; there is no such thing as a natural market as was recently demonstrated by David Greaber in his book *Debt: The First 5,000 Years*, 2012). We may want material resources at our disposal to be put into fighting cancer or getting rid of world hunger and not into developing 3D touch technology for smartphone screens or constructing fuel inefficient luxury cars, however, we have no control over how these resources are used, because they remain completely in private control. Should it be so if our collective fate depends on it? For the liberals – yes, because private property is the cornerstone of society and it originates from individual achievements. For the progressives – no, because control over material production is in the interest of entire community – or even humanity as such – and the individual property derives ultimately from some form of arbitrary privatisation or exploitation, be it either common natural resources plundered by multinational corporations or the collective effort of workers exploited by owners.

How do these two models of participation – the liberal and the progressive – function in practice? The liberal one is much more widespread and better known. It's a common wisdom that citizens should participate in public life, form associations and engage in solving social problems along the institutions of political society. This is, however, a normal mode of social and political life. The liberal idea of participation has got a flavor of social progress, but only in some particular places – like in the so called post-communist countries or in the post-colonial reality – where civil society has been underdeveloped for historical reasons. In highly developed countries of the capitalist core the liberal, civic mode of participation via NGOs and similar organisations with its limited scope remains a part of the status quo and for this reason is regarded by the progressive activists rather as part of the problem than a solution. Their progressive ideas of deeper, wider, and more intense forms of participation are less known, but also more promising in terms of future developments. For this reason I'll confine a brief overview of the practical instances of participation to the examples coming from the field of radical and progressive activism.

Making participation work: occupations

A widely used and relatively well known form of radical, progressive participation is the strategy of occupation. In some respects it resembles an older tradition of active occupational strike: workers declare a strike, they stay within the factory, but they continue production, running the plant according to their opinions. However, occupations are aimed at different milieus – mainly the public spaces and educational institutions, like universities, which brings to mind another tradition of political activism: the sit-ins movement of the 1950s and 1960s.

What makes the Occupy movement interesting and inspiring from a progressive point of view is not only its ideological content, but also its organisational form. Alain Badiou, commenting on the events of 2011 in his book *Le réveil de l'histoire* (2011), underlined the importance of this practical aspect. The point the activists tried to make was not to articulate certain demands *vis-à-vis* existing power structures or to complement them with grassroots civic activism aimed at resolving concrete problems. This way the Occupy movement does not fit into the liberal framework of civil society. What was more important was to enact in a mini-scale possible procedures and power mechanisms of future society. The clue to the occupation strategy, as Badiou put it, lies in a direct control that a group of people exercises over a piece of public space. The occupied space becomes a laboratory of the future in what has been called 'prefigurative politics' and boils down to creating a small scale version of the organisational frames of possible future politics (see Carl Boggs, 'Marxism, Prefigurative Communism, and the Problem of Workers' Control', 1977; and Nick Srnicek and Alex Williams, *Inventing the Future: Postcapitalism and a World Without Work*, 2015).

Once the occupation areas were established, concrete democratic mechanisms of self-organisation and self-management were being implemented. The most important of them is the participatory practice of so called 'General Assembly' – a daily reunion of all whom it may concern devised to discuss whatever needs to be discussed and to take decisions by majority voting. Everyone is entitled to speak out, there are no representatives and no superior authority, only a group designated to practically organise and moderate the rally. They are usually called the 'Facilitation Team' and have no actual power beyond tasks like maintaining a list of speakers, counting votes, making sure eventual conflicts are resolved in a peaceful way, etc. The assembly's participants are alert regarding any abuses of power by the facilitators. (This brief description is based on my participatory observation of Occupy Wall Street that I conducted in New York in October 2011).

What is very interesting is the performative aspect of the movement. The assemblies are vivid and dynamic events, very different from usual sessions of parliaments, where boring speeches of most MPs are met with the yawning of others. There is a system of simple hand gestures used to express basic opinions like 'I'm in favour', 'I'm against', 'I'm not decided', 'I'll absolutely oppose the move', or 'Wrap it up, you are taking too long'. They are used to provide a speaker with immediate feedback, so everyone can see what the majority opinion is (if there is one). In the case of complex issues that are difficult to debate in a general forum, there is a 10-15 minute break before voting during which everyone is encouraged to discuss the problem in small groups with their direct neighbours in the assembly.

What emerges from these sessions is a peculiar image of a multitude of subjects engaged in constant exchange. It's like a self-managing and self-regulating swarm. The feeling is amplified by oft-used voice technique called the 'human microphone': people sitting closer to the speaker repeat her sentences in short series, so people further away can hear what is being said. The operation is repeated in waves so the word can spread around the entire assembly (see Ashley Norris, 'Occupy Wall St – Human Microphone', on YouTube, 2011; and Jan Sowa, 'Les hommes et femmes de la démocratie. La multitude en tant que sujet des révolutions démocratique', 2014). This technique is used by activists to overcome a ban on loud speakers and sometimes to jam megaphones that police or other authorities may have on the site. It's surprisingly effective in this respect, showing the strength of hundreds of voices united.

The choice of public spaces – and not factories or government offices – for the occupation is not a random one. The key issue brought up by the Occupy movement is that of the commons (see Gigi Roggero, 'Roggero, 'Five Theses on the Common', 2010) – various kinds of resources and goods that should be made available to everyone, but are instead enclosed and used in the interests of the few. Examples include both material and immaterial commons: city space dominated by real estate developers and other private interests or scientific knowledge imprisoned in an ever growing system of patents, copyrights, paywalls, etc.

What is redefined here is the very notion of 'the public'. It may be said that 'the common' comes as a radical, much more participatory replacement for the liberal 'public', as the latter has become a deceptive term masking alienation underneath a formally inclusive system. The difference boils down to refusal of participation in the liberal, parliamentary sense. Its critiques believe it puts public goods and resources not under the control of the people, but of alienated members of parliament and governmental bodies, depriving the public of what is their rightful possession: the commons.

Participation is seen in the frame of Occupy movement as a way of overcoming alienation that is formally inclusive, but practically exclusive of the liberal democratic system that representation entails. Michael Hardt and Antonio Negri in their insightful book *Declaration* (2012), devoted to the events of 2011, claim that what the Occupy movement opposes in general is alienation of contemporary capitalist societies epitomised in four subjective positions: the indebted, the mediatised, the securitised, and the represented. It's worth noting in the present context that two of these predicaments – mediation and representation – refer directly to the question of participation, or rather, to the lack of it.

An interlude: occupy art!

What makes the Occupy movement very interesting given the theme of this book, is its resonance within the artistic community. A group of artists and activists associated with 16 Beaver – an artist-run space in lower Manhattan located a couple of hundred metres from the New York Stock Exchange (NYSE) – was directly engaged in the practical preparation and running of the occupation of Liberty Plaza close to the NYSE. A renowned American artist, Martha Rosler, created a series of pictures documenting a myriad of Occupy initiatives in the United States and in Europe and expressed her support for the movement in an article called 'The Artistic Mode of Revolution: From Gentrification to Occupation' published by the online art journal *E-flux* (2012). Occupy activists were invited by to take part in the 7th Berlin Biennale of Contemporary Art in 2012, which was curated by Artur Żmijewski. There are many more examples requiring a separate, more systematic study.

Interesting things happened in the theatre world as well. In many places around the world art activists decided to vindicate public theatres, believed to be an important part of the common wealth, and attempted their occupation by transforming them into institutions of the common. The best known examples from Europe include Valle Theater in Rome and Embros in Athens (see Joanna Panagiotopoulou, 'Embros Theatre', in *The Occupied Times*, 2014). I'll briefly focus on the first of them for the sake of illustration.

Occupation of Teatro Valle started in 2011 in response to the plans of privatisation of the theatre made by the municipal authorities. The historical status of Teatro Valle played an important role – it is considered a part of common cultural heritage (it was established in 1726 and has also been used as an opera house) so the idea for its privatisation provoked a public anger. The activists decided to occupy the space and to convert it into a theatre of the commons, run and supervised by a democratic collective. They expressed their political position in a statement posted on their web page: 'We are interested in commons, mutualism, co-working and we would like to base all the actions on the quality of relationships. We believe in a world built on bottom up quality processes' (Jay Walljasper, 'Theater Belongs to the People: Occupying Rome's Teatro Valle', 2014).

The experiment proved successful in terms of keeping the theatre open and providing it with a quality programme. As it was once observed by Igor Stokfiszewski, what proved to be the most difficult was devising a new, participatory, and democratic way of creating stage content. Not in terms of allowing people to influence programming by having their say in who gets to put what on stage, but in terms of actual artistic creation. The former was successfully realised, the latter, despite some experiments, was not fully satisfying and never really worked. Despite a progressive, participatory organisational form, most of the actual artistic content, although democratically programmed, was traditional and individual realisations.

It is a paradoxical development. Despite a romantic vision of artistic creation as utterly individual, every creative act is in many respects collective. It can only happen in a network of communicating singularities, where ideas get elaborated in a circulation among a number of subjects, hence the importance of milieus and groups for artistic creation. However, it looks like these new artistic creations, although generated by a multitude, can be realised in the most interesting form only by separate individuals. It makes art similar to football, where goals come as a result of collective effort, but can only actually be scored only by individuals. Interestingly enough, it is not the only resemblance between art and sport, as both domains function according to the rule of 'the winner takes all': the gap separating the best from the mediocre is much wider than the one between, let's say, the best and just ordinary plumbers, taxi drivers, teachers, and even academics. It may be the key condition to explain failed attempts at participation in artistic creation, this is, however, a separate issue requiring its own investigation.

Making participation work: workers democracy and participatory budgeting

The Occupy movement is neither the first nor maybe even the most important example of participatory practices, so I'll briefly ponder two lesser known forms of progressive participation: workers' democracy and participatory budgeting.

The idea that the workplace should be collectively controlled by the workers is very old, actually older than the industrial production that it is usually associated with. The first known attempts to enact workers' democracy – control over both day to day functioning of a given organisation and of distribution of profits deriving from undertaken activities – were introduced on... pirate ships! However strange it may sound to our righteous ears, pirates were the first to systematically introduce very participative and democratic management of their workplaces: on many vessels, captains were elected and important decisions outside of the battlefield had to be taken by majority voting including the crucial question of how to split the loot (see Peter Linebaugh and Marcus Rediker, *The Many-Headed Hydra: Sailors, Slaves, Commoners, and the Hidden History of the Revolutionary Atlantic*, 2000; and Peter Lamborn Wilson, *Pirate Utopias: Moorish Corsairs & European Renegadoes*, 2003). As a result, pirate communities were quite equal on a material level:

31

'management' of the ship – meaning the captain and his (or hers, as pirates were also progressive when it came to gender and accepted women within their ranks, even as captains) aids – could receive a maximum of twice the amount given to a regular crew members.

The workers' control had been enacted and tested on many occasions in more 'standard' circumstances. It proved practical and efficient in purely material terms. Many factories owned and controlled by workers functioned at least as efficiently as they did before in private hands. The most famous examples are probably the Zanon ceramic factory on the outskirts of Buenos Aires in Argentina and the Flasko chemical plant near Campinas in Brazil (see Esteban Magnani, *The Silent Change: Recovered Businesses in Argentina*, 2009; and Avi Lewis and Naomi Klein (dir.), *The Take*, 2004). They sometimes produce cheaper products and always provide better wages for the workers, however the benefits go far beyond the question of income. A very important aspect of participation is a liberating feeling of agency among workers that leads not only to better performance, but also to their healthier psychic functioning. They do not feel alienated and even if they have to make sacrifices to keep the factory running by working overtime or earning less for the sake of necessary investments, they feel it is their decision that would also benefit them in the long run.

The practice of participatory budgeting is a form of progressive participation being implemented in many cities around the world, however mostly in its very limited form, where only a small fraction of city's budget is distributed via participatory mechanisms and citizens' projects even if voted for realisation can always be cancelled by the city administration as 'unfeasible' or 'undesired' for some reasons (for example, many cyclists' initiatives in Warsaw were struck down despite being voted as harmful for the circulation of cars).

The broadest experiment with participatory budgeting has been undertaken in the Brazilian city of Porto Alegre since late 1980s, where most of city's budget was shaped in a participatory way. A process of long and complicated negotiations is starting in neighbourhoods and goes through districts, ending on a city-wide level. The potential investments are first put forward by citizens themselves and later voted by them. The endeavour includes representatives but they are bound by instructions from their constituencies in the way described earlier in this text (see Yves Sintomer, Carsten Herzberg, and Anja Röcke, 'Participatory Budgeting in Europe: Potentials and Challenges', 2008). Any experts involved in the process play a menial and humble role of helping people do, in the fullest possible sense, what people want to do. It stands in stark contrast to the neoliberal culture of experts, where they are mostly used to persuade people why what the latter want – more public services and their better accessibility, more redistribution, more social justice, higher wages, etc. – cannot be achieved.

The case of participatory budgeting reveals one of the biggest problems in any attempt to construct participatory political mechanisms. They are very demanding in terms of time and energy that they require to function: only an ongoing engagement of a considerable part of population can keep them alive. This is, however, very difficult in the long run. Enthusiasm is crucial, but as we all know, initiatives propelled by enthusiasm are as spectacular as they are short lived. As it was observed in a mean, however pertinent way by Oscar Wilde, socialism is a great system, but we would have to sacrifice too many free evenings to make it happen. Everyday life, with its imperative to work at least eight hours a day, makes it very difficult to be an engaged citizen at the same time. The Ancient Greeks understood it perfectly well and for this reason they believed that only individuals in possession of slaves and thus liberated from obligation to labour can participate in public life in any meaningful way. Parliamentarism has got the incredible advantage of being not very time consuming. It is enough to sacrifice half an hour every four years to be an 'active' citizen. It lasts also because it is convenient and corresponds well with limitations of our semi-emancipated societies. Any attempt to transform general society in a more participative way requires a fundamental remodelling of our social contract and the introduction of some kind of guaranteed basic income. It would free up some of our time and allow us to be not only workers and consumers, but participating citizens as well.

DOMINIQUE NDUHURA

TO PARTICIPATE OR NOT TO PARTICIPATE

A CLOSER LOOK INTO FORUM THEATRE AND FREEDOM OF EXPRESSION IN AFRICA

Theatre in Africa is one of the oldest means of communication which predates the mass media and on which colonisation relied heavily to pass on Western ideologies. Traditional theatre making had to adjust to new theatre from the West. Many embraced theatre for its diverse virtues especially for tackling development issues, which is why it was largely referred to as Theatre for Development. Batilloi Warritay argues that theatre has the ability to help defuse conflictual situations in an amicable way. Theatre has the potential to create critical consciousness among the people towards problems in their environment, hence triggering change. This becomes possible especially as theatre has an intrinsic value of participation. Participatory theatre relies on local languages to help communities understand development messages in a simpler way and certainly at low cost. In their study entitled 'Women's Voices and African Theatre: Case studies from Kenya, Mali, The Democratic Republic of Congo and Zimbabwe' (2003), Article 19 sustained that:

> Theatre is the only art form in which the whole human being is actually employed as the instrument for expressing or investigating the human condition. As a result, it allows for a dichotomising of the self, or objectification of reality, so that human beings can observe themselves in action. This act of seeing oneself allows one to envision alternatives – particularly since theatre is in its essence a communal activity, which facilitates a sharing of knowledge and experience that may lead to it becoming a rehearsal for change.

35

As such, theatre on the African continent has always been used for entertainment and beyond. The most recurrent messages covered in this theatre include health, religion, education, politics, social, or economic issues. Many believe that theatre for development gained its full potential when it started espousing participatory and liberatory philosophies from Paolo Freire and his student Augusto Boal with his *Theatre of the Oppressed* (1993). The latter was conceived to become a means of resistance for the people in general, and the most vulnerable social categories in particular. Boal wanted his theatre to be a transformational forum for people's self-expression which leads to empowerment, both at individual and collective levels. Forum theatre, which is the core of this paper, is one type that subscribes to Boal's framework of popular theatre.

Although forum theatre has been adapted to fit to local contexts where it was applied, its initial idea lies in showing a play to audience members – referred to by Boal as 'spect-actors' – with a 'joker' who serves as a facilitator. Audience members are free to interrupt the play at any stage in order to step in and showcase how they think oppression should be dealt with. In that sense, the gap between performers and audiences that generally characterises classical theatre is broken. In its initial stages, forum theatre was meant to be a game changer against political oppression. In his assessment of community theatre's efficacy in the South African context, Kennedy C. Chinyowa explains that forum theatre presents an 'anti-model' who is looked at as the oppressor and who is targeted by protagonists as the play rolls out in a bid to find a solution to the source of oppression.

A plethora of researchers and reports have proven too laudatory by hailing the potential and the benefits that forum theatre generates in different settings despite some challenges inherent to any cultural production. The most recurrent field on the continent that amply harnessed forum theatre is certainly the fight against HIV/AIDS. UNESCO's toolkit, 'Act, Learn and Teach: Theatre, HIV and AIDS Toolkit for Youth in Africa', offers one optimistic outlook of why and how forum theatre should be used in fighting epidemics. This organisation emphasises that forum theatre has the merit to be an equaliser in that it allows all audience members – without exclusion – to voice their needs and shape together their destiny. In his region-wide analysis entitled 'Art and Conscientization: Forum Theatre in Uganda, Rwanda, DR Congo, and South Sudan' (2015), Claus Schrowange warns against the tendency of some to reduce forum theatre to mere entertainment. Instead, he believes that when

Magnet Theatre performing in a village near Malindi, Kenya, 2006

forum theatre is used 'in a participatory manner with an authentic, believable acting style, involving both the audience and stage actor in a vivid and touching experience, the impact is immediately felt'.

Many more researchers welcomed warmly the use of forum theatre for HIV/AIDS eradication which, up to now, seems to be the kernel of Entertainment-Education (EE) initiatives. Paulin Basinga et al found that, when used along with other classical education methods, forum theatre played a major role in increasing youth's self-efficacy and readiness to use prevention methods, thus contributing largely to behavioural change among secondary school adolescents in Rwanda. In the same vein, in his analysis on how to use forum theatre to promote youth's awareness of reproductive health-related problems including HIV/AIDS education, Dennis Francis elaborates that forum theatre has an invaluable potential to create openness and assertiveness, which are key steps in behaviour change in the context of HIV/AIDS. Used as a Problem Solving Project, forum theatre was found to be useful in a factory environment. Emma Durden and Dominique Nduhura's analysis revealed that forum theatre presents a promising opportunity to the workplace where it allows engaging the audience in the drama process; raises awareness about HIV and AIDS; and empowers communities to talk about this epidemic.

Forum theatre was used for many more purposes. In a different study on the use of forum theatre in fighting heterosexism and heteronormativity in a South African education, Francis discusses that this tool presents very satisfactory results. However, he is fast to nuance that forum theatre by itself would not liberate communities as there still subsists hindrances such as socialisation, privilege, and local context. The same optimism transpires from Nehemia Chivandikwa and Ngonidzashe Muwonwa's analysis that concludes that forum theatre in Zimbabwe constitutes a privileged place to debate topics that in Africa are generally considered as taboo or very complex, such as sexuality and disability.

In 'Theatre for Development and Northern Uganda: An Avenue for Hope? Or a Lofty Ambition?' (2005) Nandita Dinesh noted rosy results in conflict resolution where forum theatre brings communities to learn from each other, thus quelling the differences among them. Most importantly, forum theatre helped communities to interact and encouraged them to participate instead of using traditional top-down methods. Dinesh argues that, through interactions:

> Forum theatre promotes a higher-order questioning and analysis that really begins to empower transformation. Individuals begin to realise that their oppressions are man-made rather than the natural order of things, and that they have the 'power within' to change that reality. Yet the true value of forum theatre as a tool for empowerment is that it is also a 'rehearsal for reality'; participants are able to actively practice the strategies and skills needed to alter the status quo in a safe-space before implementing them in real-life.

In that, forum theatre is a powerful tool through which communities are able to 'have fun and save lives'. Also, contrary to other communication tools, forum theatre can easily be taken to remote places where most African illiterate and poor populations live. On top of that, the whole process is accomplished at very low cost.

Successful achievements were also recorded in other countries such as Rwanda, Burundi, Côte d'Ivoire, and Democratic Republic of Congo (DRC) where forum theatre was used by Search for Common Ground (SFCG), a US-based organisation. Sydney

Smith and Elise Webb reported cases where SFCG used participatory theatre for initiatives such as implementation of land policy; promoting public voices of women on key societal issues; promoting entrepreneurship among the youth; unity and reconciliation; and peace and conflict resolution. More specifically, Ananda Breed highlighted SFCG success in Rwanda where forum theatre was instrumental to promoting justice and reconciliation among perpetrators and victims in the post-Genocide era.

In Tanzania, forum theatre is also very popular. The Ideas Factory was a campaign that was initiated in 2006 to try and catalyse positive change in youth by including them in decision making, social entrepreneurship, and civic education. The campaign aimed at drastically transforming youth's attitudes in order to bring younger generations to aim high and prepare to sculpt their destinies and their society's. Social transformation was also at the heart of Ikusasa Lakho (2006), a theatre project in South Africa which aimed to change the youth whose past was tarnished by colonialism and apartheid.

Worth noting also is the big number of projects based on drama for education and behaviour change on the continent, in which forum theatre was the cornerstone. These projects include for instance DramAidE which has used various participatory methods for HIV/AIDS education in South Africa since 1992; the Marotholi Traveling Theatre in Lesotho (1982–85); the Theatre for Integrated rural Development Programme in Sierra Leone (in the 1980s); Amakhosi Academy of Performing Arts in Zimbabwe (1981); experiments by the Department of English at the University de Yaounde, Cameroun (in the 1980s); the Kasama Theatre Arts Production of Zambia (1993); a UNICEF Theatre for Development project (2015); and a Johns Hopkins University – (PCS) – Adolescent Fertility project in Nigeria (in the 1980s), amongst others.

Although communication experts and drama practitioners were many among those purporting forum theatre's appropriateness to the field of entertainment and education in African contexts, others have noted very important challenges. Many tend to blame the process, finding it too lengthy in most cases as it is not granted for community members (referred to earlier as spect-actors) to easily reach a solution to the problem at hand. In addition, from the experience of the DramAidE project in South Africa, it has turned out that forum theatre's audience is not the same in different sessions. As a result, performers may find themselves in situations where their influence on the audience happens just once, hence it

Elijah Njenga and europuppet. Njenga as narrator mediates between the audience and puppets. Kibera slums, Nairobi, Kenya, 2006

is neither continuous nor sustainable enough to trigger the requisite awareness and behaviour change. In other cases, forum theatre proved to have unexpected effects. For instance, it happened sometimes that audiences practice the bad ideas they watch in drama instead of following positive role models. These community members are curious to discover by themselves whether the ideas – positive or negative – displayed in the play could work in real life.

Dinesh highlights that in countries with multiple ethnic groups – hence different languages – it has always been daunting for performance groups to communicate with local communities. In the same context, skepticism has been noted when forum theatre was performed in the presence of different groups who have diverging views, especially regarding conflicts. People are also afraid to implement the lessons learnt from forum theatre due to non-supportive environments, and this applies to different contexts such as health, security/war, or any other social issue. In addition, artists are not always open to performing in some remote areas for safety fears.

To other theatre experts, even the concept of participation at the heart of forum theatre is not clearly defined. Durden points to the fact that, although it is useful for behaviour change, participation in drama might be problematic especially when there is influence from funders. Often times, drama projects appear to put forward participation in theory, but in reality, the process is manned by an outside agency that targets its own objectives – sometimes at odds with people's priorities – and, at the end of the day the projects are just another way to teach the community in a top-down approach. Audiences are not given the freedom to orient the play the way they want and do not have freedom to divert the key messages which are imposed to them by funders.

Critically reflecting on the work done through Laedza Batanani (1974) (roughly meaning 'community awakening'), a non-formal education project in Botswana which was built on the Freirian pedagogy, Ross Kidd and Martin Byram first acknowledged this project's potential to encouraging participation, raising issues, fostering discussion, and promoting collective action, but also its capacity to propagate dominant class ideas and inducing acceptance of the status quo. Hence, this pseudo-participatory theatre was found to be more domesticating than liberating as it is the initial idea from Freire and Boal.

Institutionalisation of forum theatre is therefore one key problem which subjects drama to agendas set by local context. Hence, forum theatre is highly impeded by lack of freedom of expression. Topics addressed are those that are in line with governments' policies, whereas disturbing issues are left aside, even when they are at the heart of social oppression, and especially in cases where the latter is imputable to local Governments. In other words, forum theatre and other types of participatory theatre tend to be used more as tools of domestication than positive transformation based on real needs of the people.

Institutionalisation of forum theatre is detrimental to practitioners' free work. Frances Rifkin highlighted that practitioners are not able to freely 'set working methods; agree agendas with participants; choose and develop ways of working; evaluate in appropriate ways; and work creatively with notions of uncertainty, bewilderment and discovery'. Practitioners are forced to adhere to ethics and standards set by funders, who in general do not really understand either how drama should work or what audiences' needs should be prioritised. As a result, practitioners are overlooked by the powerful, which substantially hampers the quality of forum theatre.

41

Over time, participatory theatre became just a buzz word cherished by many African politicians and other decision-makers whose main objective was to show that their actions are meant for the people, yet implementation borrowed a rather top-down model. In Ghana, Okagbu reported a penchant by government representatives to publicly boast of supporting participatory theatre whereas they thwarted projects that supported participatory processes. The same tendency was found in Uganda and Tanzania. Frances Harding noticed that the government and other influential organisations in the country supported theatre for development in theory, for instance in HIV/AIDs projects. But the reality was different. These organisations were more interested in quantifiable data – number of performances, number of spectators, number of participants – than the process, i.e. quality of participation and the actual impact of the project. Therefore, many drama projects claimed to be participatory whereas they focused on putting out the message and evaluating the results, hence falling into the didactic trap. By doing so, they fool the funders who keep pumping in money, especially since they do not necessarily understand the difference between participatory and conventional theatre; they base their decisions of whether to fund or not on monitoring and evaluations that in general tend to paint a favourable picture of projects.

Whether or not they understand the scope and nature of participatory theatre, decision-makers have always swayed on participatory processes in order to pass on their ideologies in a paternalistic way. This was the case especially during the colonial era where, for instance, the British government used to commission cultural products such as theatre. Drama was therefore meant to educate and civilise poor and illiterate masses in the countryside. From the independence wave in the 1960s and up to the 1980s, participatory drama was ambivalent. On the one hand, theatre for development was used as a political weapon by groups that fought colonisation and subsequent dictatorships. On the other hand, most African governments tended to engulf and censor theatre in fear of its revolutionary potential. The situation worsened when from the 1980s, most African countries struggled against Structural Adjustment Programmes imposed by the International Monetary Fund (IMF), hence cutting off funds forecast for lower priority sectors such as culture. In this crisis, control over development theatre fell into the hands of international organisations for the major part. As a result, the latter used theatre as a way to pass Western ideologies onto African countries, thus overlooking the voices from local communities.

By controlling the messages disseminated through participatory theatre, paymasters automatically shaped its methodology. Throughout the 1980s, 1990s and the 2000s, many projects were implemented with a main focus on HIV/AIDS. International agencies and governments widely censored even basic information such as the 'Abstinence, Be faithful and use Condom' (ABC) slogan. Some governments and charities did not support the use of condoms, which brought many people to die from the epidemic. Funders swayed on methodology in as far as – to paraphrase Jane Plastow – they no longer commissioned plays, but invested in training facilitators and performers by instilling in them new techniques to be used in different communities. This new way of doing theatre for development bore substantial weaknesses since no community resembles another, and techniques which work in one community do not necessarily apply to another. In so doing, funding agencies used theatre for development as an alibi to propagate their ideologies. For instance, Plastow noted the 'wave of homophobia' that invaded Uganda as a result of Western agencies interested in disseminating their own views rather than pursuing local people's priorities.

As it appears, there is always a gap between theory and practice. Participatory theatre in Africa is said to be driven by local communities, whereas the upper hand from the government and other funders is unavoidable. Consequently, the potential of so-called participatory theatre is heavily impacted on and the projects lose their ability to generate long-lasting change. However, some scholars have a penchant for supporting a paternalistic view in drama projects. Amongst other drama experts, Zakes Mda argues that communities need to be guided in their choice of solutions to their problems by an external intervention for the optimal attainment of projects objectives.

As I contend in this paper, politics was gradually abandoned by drama practitioners in Africa, thus paving way to other topics deemed to be less 'dangerous', such as education, health, or any other lighter subjects. Playmakers shied away from confronting governments by unearthing very sensitive areas such as corruption at all levels; pervasive injustice; arbitrary killings and other human rights violations; increasing inequalities between the rich and the poor; poor management of various institutions; and a recent tendency for Heads of States to change their country's constitutions in order to cling to power. Such topics have progressively become no-go-zones in many African countries, yet they form the main maladies that keep most African countries rotting in poverty.

In reality, the abovementioned sensitive topics form core sources of citizens' oppression in the Freirean sense.

Mass media and any other forms of communication are under perpetual scrutiny by governments, most of which do not tolerate dissent voices. Freedom of expression is always at its lowest in many African countries. International bodies such as Reporters without Borders, Freedom House, and Human Rights paint a negative picture of many countries year in year out. Journalists are killed, harassed or forced into exile. UNESCO has recently noted some efforts to promote freedom of expression in Africa such as media pluralism and legal reforms. However, in many countries, these efforts remained futile since most governments are still inclined to systematically mute critical voices. In the past few years, there was a trend to transform state-controlled broadcasters into public broadcasters, but all this has shown poor results. Governments have maintained a culture of secrecy and media professionals are pushed to always practise self-censorship while populations in general are not allowed to fully exercise their rights to freedom of expression. At the same time, media activists and civil society are reduced to silence. For the last six to seven years, Freedom House has been assessing African countries in terms of freedom of expression and has classified a great number of them as 'not free' and 'partly free'.

In such an unfriendly context, forum theatre, much as it is conceived of as liberatory and revolutionary by many, would not dare venture into creating critical consciousness and praxis without otherwise falling out with governments. On the contrary, Article 19 sustains that theatre in general is key to freedom of expression. Participatory theatre has even more power to contribute to the right to free expression since it thrives to give voice to the voiceless, such as women and other vulnerable groups, by allowing them to achieve a consensual solution to their problems.

What is at stake therefore is the uneasy and ever changing relationship between communication forms, including participatory theatre, and politics in the African context. Back in the colonial times, the colonial authorities controlled and banned theatre for development which they feared would increase local consciousness against colonization. After independence, theatre was widely used to celebrate independence and build nationalism through government propaganda. At the same time, it was used by those who opposed governments, thus triggering the anger of the authorities. In some countries like Tanzania, participating in theatre production was considered a crime unless authorised by the government, and a

Audience at Kibera slums, Nairobi, Kenya, 2006

Stage Plays Authority was created for this effect. In South Africa, theatre was instrumental in the fight against Apartheid, while in Uganda theatre was at the core of the anti-Idi Amin propaganda. In Kenya, *I Will Marry When I Want* (1977) was one famous political play by Ngugi wa Thiong'o and Ngugi wa Miri. In Nigeria and other countries, popular theatre played an important role in fighting dictatorship from the 1970s up until the 1990s by exposing corruption, among other things. Some few countries such as South Africa went on showing openness to participatory theatre where political satire was produced to criticise the process of peace and reconciliation. More recently, Arab countries such as Morocco, Tunisia, and Egypt tended to freely tolerate the practice of theatre, especially after the Arab Spring. As notes Cleo Jay, participatory theatre flourished during and after the 'Arab Spring' where theatre practitioners took to the internet and social media to promote their plays by reaching out to the youth. In so doing, theatre and performance played a key role in the revolution by liberating and empowering the youth.

Giant puppet (animated by Michael Mutahi), that is used to summon audience, and Peter Mutie with microphone. Kibera slums, Nairobi, Kenya, 2006

However, popular theatre went through many hardships including extremely hostile political and economic conditions in which some of the best playwrights were forced into exile, for example Wole Soyinka and Ngugi wa Thiongo. When the latter eventually returned to Kenya, he saw his play *Mother, Cry for Me* banned as it was deemed too critical towards the government. Censorship subsists in theatre in most African countries. Censorship and self-censorship are key limitations in most countries with weak freedom of expression. In Uganda, Dinesh notes that when artists and audiences are faced with political issues that may cause trouble, they prefer to overlook such topics. Interviewed by *What's on Africa Nowadays*, some younger play writers from South Africa claimed to enjoy much more freedom than in many other African countries. They however deplored difficulty in writing on some topics, for instance political corruption. Theatre is censored albeit to a lesser extent and with less ease as compared to other forms of mainstream media. In Malawi, play writers work in hazardous conditions where governments strictly censor theatre. In North Africa, participatory theatre was censored by governments, which deprived play writers from their power to criticise and help topple regimes as it was the case during the Arab Spring. In Cameroun, Ambroise Kom discusses that censorship in this country reduced play writers to silence, or if not, drama productions dwelt on rather trivial topics where politics would hardly surface.

In a nutshell, participatory theatre in Africa has numberless benefits for development and democracy. It can build the capacity of individuals; create community harmony; give voice to vulnerable populations; promote dialogue; and promote common action. No doubt about this. However, things tend to go astray due to theatre ownership. In general, theatre in Africa is managed by governments or other funding agencies who find in it an easy and cheap means to propagate their ideologies by overlooking local populations' deep-rooted needs. As such, owners dictate what participation should be, thus controlling the whole process of theatre and messages. Ironically, it turns out that governments and development agencies, knowingly or unknowingly, always claim to be guided by participation in all their endeavors. Participation has become a buzzword in political discourse. Participatory theatre was therefore hijacked by some to defend their own interests, hence succumbing under censorship, which is a key pattern in the communication sphere of most African countries. Participatory theatre has turned mild as topics are no longer disturbing. Play writers would not dare bite the hand that feeds them. Instead, topics addressed are mostly meant to promote health, education, fighting gender-based violence, and many more 'soft' areas. On the other side, people tend to participate just to please implementers (façade participation). Thus, marred by lack of freedom, forum theatre, and so-called development theatre in general, seems to have shifted from the Theatre of the Oppressed logic, as it was Boal's initial philosophy, to become rather theatre of the oppressor, or at least, theatre of the powerful.

ANTOINE PICKELS

LET ME PARTICIPATE

AND I'LL
TELL YOU
WHO I AM

Participation in the arts is definitely in the air – it has even become a leitmotif of cultural orthodoxy. For some years now, the idea has triggered interest in both the practice and the aesthetics of visual arts, where this issue in particular was theorised by Nicolas Bourriaud (*Relational Aesthetics*, 1998) or Paul Ardenne (*Un art contextuel* [*A Contextual Art*], 2002). Since the 1960s and 1970s, participation has been one of the tools of performance art, where the 'witness of the action' element is often constitutive of the work. Finally, it is one of those classic 'tricks' deployed by street artists, some of whom are now developing more experimental forms.

More recently, participation has also made a remarkable comeback in the questionings – and in the productions – of theatre and of dance, where it had not been operative for some period. What is therein at play is a certain fashion and sometimes-artificial devices; yet, perhaps, also a genuine yearning for society that manifests itself elsewhere than in the world of performing arts. Yet, before we dwell on recent theatrical and choreographic expressions of this phenomenon, let's first see how participation plays (out) in the three other above-mentioned artistic spheres.

From the periphery to the core
The artistic practices in the so-called *esthétique relationnelle* in the French-speaking world, also referred to as public art and socially engaged art in the English-speaking world, were widely touted in the 1990s, assuming a larger dimension in the early 2000s. These arose both as a rejection of the art marketplace by some artists, and likewise an attempt by those very same artists to restore politics to a social space where ideologies were lacking. And yet, they

would not have flourished to any great extent without the will of the political powers, who sought to legitimise the state's cultural funding policy with artworks going 'in front of people', and to eventually heal by dint of art the wounds of a society whose social bonds were disintegrating, in synch with the advances of neoliberalism. If some outstanding creative works (and subsequently, artistic careers) thus emerged, they rarely earned their authors recognition from the world of the domineering art, namely, the marketplace. Nevertheless, they did gain acceptance in this 'second' world of art, that is in art education, research, or even as beneficiaries of public commissions, which today afford artists access to less lucrative, albeit in themselves rewarding, creative paths. The cultural foundations that spawn multiple collectors in parallel with their activities, or educational activities at museums or art centres (themselves often infiltrated by private collectors or the corporate world) nowadays sponsor participatory works for identical reasons that the state used to subsidise them in the past: primarily as an alibi. And, artists who initially evolved in theatre and dance also operate within these structures, where pressure from this other market – in the form of the scenic arts – is non-existent.

In the world of performance art, participation has been commonplace since the 1960s. At this level there is a continuum between the feminist *Cut Piece* by Yoko Ono in 1964 (where the artist invited audience members to cut away her clothing piece by piece with a pair of scissors), the cuts (made by an audience member on a one-to-one basis) into the skin of the UK-based artist Kira O'Reilly in her body performances of the late 1990s and early 2000s, or the more metaphorical performance-streams that the Chilean Alejandra Herrera Silva is currently producing (that inevitably involve using one or more audience members to perform the ritual). Numerous performances, enacted exclusively by the audience, have also seen the disappearance of the artist's physical presence. This is, in fact, one of the challenges of performance art, namely, that of abolishing barriers between actor and spectator. Spontaneous or forced participation is one means of getting there, if not the only (shifting the story-telling towards a more personal register, interweaving the space or stretching time could, for example, seek a comparable effect). If performance art is historically a marginal and peripheral practice, it has nonetheless attracted renewed interest both among the public and artists... especially since the internet's popularisation. It is as though the almost constant presence in our daily lives of that media filter and relationships at a distance have given, by contrast, greater relevance to an art of the here-and-now as well as of the unique and non-reproducible moment. The scenic arts, in particular, pay it considerable attention ever since the 'post-dramatic' has become a religion, and Jacques Rancière's *The Emancipated Spectator* (2009) the most quoted text in contemporary theatrical and choreographic circles.

What was once dubbed street theatre or fairground theatre, and now being labelled as 'performing art in public space' (the shift in the terminology is revealing) has always hinged upon onlooker participation – as was the case with some music hall acts, like magic. These onlookers, whom it's a matter of drawing in, if we want to win their attention in the distracting and 'entertaining' space that is the street, have happily played along down through the centuries. For this was always seen as part of the distractions on offer in social space, amusements one expects at a fair or at the market, being assailed by a vendor of 'miracle' household goods, discount vegetables merchants, or by a street-artist performing his number. For modern onlookers, well versed in Web 2.0, social networking and online petitions, participation goes beyond this tradition to become a genuine right to be exercised. It is not just a matter of accepting to be exploited, but the spectacle affords them the impression of having 'their say', of being co-authors of the work... without, however, that their contribution be too demanding. In ways similar to how we identify with a collective flag, or whatever the 'Je suis...' of the moment is on Facebook. Street performers (who themselves are users of the same social networks) need to bear in mind this sociological evolution in their offerings. It is noteworthy that aesthetic values have also shifted in the art milieu operative in public space, occupied by artists forsaking fortresses steeped in 'indoor' theatre and dance, or by better-trained circus performers, and hence, equipped with more refined dramaturgical skills... The production and distribution networks have also become much more professional. This shift was particularly made possible in Europe by means of the international grant programmes, ideally suited to these nomadic and essentially 'completely public' forms. In these powerful networks, such as In Situ or Circostrada, far removed from the 'has been' image once attributed to street arts, participation has now become a buzzword.

All these practices, essentially (dis)considered as somewhat peripheral, have recently been the subject of revaluation; the existence of aesthetic-political credos like those of Rancière and the significance, at least in the media, of innovative insurgent political movements (and with greater 'horizontal' participation) such as the Arab Spring, *los Indignados*, Occupy, *Nuit debout* to name but a few, have now suddenly made concepts and practices that seemed out-dated since the phlegmatic 1980s acceptable in the spheres of High Art. Furthermore, the most dominant sectors of 'indoors' dance and theatre, in turn, try to upstage each other with participatory proposals. Citing several examples I encountered over the course of spring 2016 in Scotland and Belgium will enable us to identify some trends.

Scenic foundations

The Buzzcut Festival, hosted by the queer artists Rosana Cade and Nick Anderson – in their creations on the fringe of Live Art and experimental theatre, they regularly seek direct public participation – takes place in the neglected neighbourhood of Govan in Glasgow, at a community centre dating from 1906, the period in which the world's largest shipyards were the city's pride. In one way or another, virtually all of the festival's offerings call for public involvement (including contributing to the costs, based on the 'pay as you can' principle that, ultimately, was more profitable than imposing a fixed price). And, in more or less traditional ways: by urging the audience to sing-along or to make noise, all while maintaining the stage-hall distinction; by summoning a spectator to carry the artist from one end of the stage to the other, or to spoon-feed an artist (Katy Dye) performing in her *Baby Face* (2016) so as to behave like a baby; for the entire audience to carry overhead the artist (Lucy McCormick, a member of Getinthebackofthevan) off-stage during a stage dive all the more impressive in that she was not wearing any panties and had just, as part of the *Easter Performance* (2016), had her genitals pawed over and licked by her partners under the pretext of the stations of the Passion; being dragged into a *Drone Dance* (2016) taking place in the game space involving four complacent spectators for a folkloric choreography directed by robot vacuum-cleaners, instigated by The Robot and Bob; or to dispose of clothing and personal effects for the *Ajima* (2013) 'freak show' performance, directed by Marc Gabriel, featuring Maija Karhunen, a dancer with an extra-ordinary physique. Afflicted with brittle-bone disease, Karhunen usually gets around in a wheelchair; here, she juggled and danced with the discarded personal effects before returning them to each spectator, accompanied with a fortune teller's prediction. So many modes of participation claiming kinship to cabaret, music hall, rock... but here reset

Buzzcut, *Easter Performance* (2016)

into a critical context assuming the spectator's intelligence (and sense of self-deprecation).

Participation assumed a more elaborate aspect in a work like *Etudes hérétiques* (2016) by Antonija Livingstone and Nadia Lauro, reinventing Plato's Symposium format (originally 'a cluster of enthusiastic pederasts') in an (overly?) protracted meditative moment, involving more than 20 citizens-cum-extras in the audience, who apparently give of themselves with pleasure towards the realisation of a queer 'living architecture', at once choreographic, musical, and sculptural. In *The Talk* (2015) by the Australian Mish Grigor, the participatory aspect succeeded, in the end, to generate a spectacular, if somewhat impromptu, theatrical highlight. In this re-enactment of family conversations dealing with sexuality, audience members chosen at random by the artist, interpreted the artist and members of her family. The scenes, which participants discover when reading them aloud, deal with parental explanations on puberty, coming-out, and then announcing the HIV status of a younger brother, awkward questions about the parent's sexuality or the indiscretions of a flirty older brother encountered on Tinder – in addition to the risqué confessions about condoms lost in the depths of Mish Grigor herself. The fact that the actors are members of the public, non-professionals, and that discussing sexuality in family is such a universal taboo created a sense of camaraderie and solidarity around this completely understandable and moving piece, in turns hilarious and serious, despite or because of the actors' inexperience... and thanks to Grigor's writing talents and improvisatory skills.

All these projects (and others, closer to the tradition of performance art involving intimate sharing on a one-on-one basis, or more unauthorised collective productions) bear similarities in how they reflect the interest of the two organisers-cum-artists for a feminist, queer de-colonised, and people with disabilities vision of society, a society where politics actually happens because we reconsider the personal aspects of our lives. Participation, often characterised by pop gimmicks ('natural' in the land of David Bowie and Freddie Mercury), was primarily an effective means of interrogating identity-related certitudes (gender, sex, 'race', physical or psychological conformity...) by demonstrating how queer, feminist, anti-colonial theories... could flourish in a societal environment (the case in point being Scotland, and Glasgow in particular) where solidarity and care remain highly valued and constantly adopting to changing circumstances.

Common good
The Buda Arts Centre in Kortrijk in Flanders is more dedicated to experimentation and artist in residence programmes than to live performance as such. At the end of April 2016, it devoted a three-day programme to 'projects based on collaboration with spectators, conversation and co-learning situations.' *What's the Matter with Cooperation?* aimed at going beyond mere 'participation' so as to identify current areas of genuine *cooperation*. Onstage, seen as an image of our society; in the city, public space being perceived as theatre with the human body as incorporating the citizen; through feedback about sharing citizen-oriented approaches in neighbourhood relationships; or, again, with tools such as open source publishing.... On the level of the participatory works presented, and while most of the propositions were meant to be playful, they struck a considerably more serious tone than those participatory happenings in Glasgow, and were less influenced by popular culture than by the values of contemporary dance.

The variations of *Building Conversation* (since 2013) that the Dutch theatre director Lotte van den Berg has been organising for some time are multiple. Unlike in her earlier overly written works,

Einer von den Jungs, die neben mir
holte zwei U-Bahn Karten raus
und hielt sie sich als Victory-Zeichen vors Gesicht.

Laila Soliman, *No Time for Art 0.0* (2012)

including the iconic *Wasteland* (2005) conceived for public spaces,
here it is a question of setting up apparently simple 'dispositives',
devices as such that leave us no option but to converse differently,
and whose deployment depends on the presence and the actions
of those participating: for example, what would happen, should we
all remain silent for three hours – and where conversation unfolds
through exchanging glances and gestures? These conversations, not
all that minimal in fact, could be, depending on the participants,
disappointing or exciting – just as conversations in real life are, after
all – but in any case opening possibilities for freedom. With a much
more elaborate score, *InsTanzen* (2014) by deufert&plischke gives
more the impression of a treasure hunt, with few opportunities
to alter the rules. Built around two pianos on which Alain Franco
and Jean-Luc Plouvier splendidly interpret the *Rite of Spring*, in a
space littered with red balloons, the spectators find on their chairs,
placed in a semi-circle, envelopes containing instructions on various
actions to perform, sometimes in response to a gesture produced
by someone else. The random juxtaposition of gestures created a
one-off choreography, obviously unique for each performance. The
tasks to be carried out by each audience member created a strange

InCompany, *Worker's Club* (2016)

tension: for one either applied oneself to the task at hand and hence created an obstacle to one's aesthetic perception as a spectator, or, one disengaged oneself completely, to suddenly find oneself guilty of detachment and of not being able to participate in the joint action.

More *laborious* – but nonetheless legitimate, because it was a question of interrogating, in the tradition of utopian space designed by Alexander Rodchenko for Art Deco in Paris in 1925, the forms and conditions of *work* – was the *Worker's Club* (2016) by Incompany (Einat Tuchman, Heike Langsdorf, and Nicolas Galeazzi). In a more congenial setting, over a bowl of soup and a glass of wine, participants were invited, according to the colour of their badge, to join a group in which various modes of collaboration sought to generate, through dialogue with co-participants but with rather more constraining devices such as an installation piece, story-telling, a performance on the body of the artist. After the results of these 'workshops' had been shared, all the spectators gathered to produce an 'exquisite corpse' from words written with a marker on large pieces of paper. These compulsory games, at once extremely controlled and regulated, gave rise to some pleasurable moments, but proved powerless to propose a counter-model to work – or that

Christophe Meierhans, *Verein zur Aufhebung des Notwendigen/ A hundred wars to world peace* (2015)

of the communist ideal. And yet, it has not been substantiated that Stakhanovism and the Soviet collective farms were in any way more fulfilling than the competition and burnout spawned by neoliberalism, manipulating desires and emotions, as was targeted by Frédéric Lordon in *Capitalisme, désir et servitude* (*Capitalism, Desire and Bondage*, 2010). Christophe Meierhans's 'culinary' and democratic project *Verein zur Aufhebung des Notwendigen – A Hundred Wars to World Peace* (2015) proved, ultimately, more convincing (and theatrical) through its restraint and shouldered frustrations. Here, beset by its contradictions, the nature of a score, demanding the strict compliance that numerous participatory works involve, triggered the absurd, laughter, and reflection. The stage was equipped with everything needed for cooking, including foodstuffs laden with contradictory 'values': an entire chunk of meat, tins of organic leeks, or kilos of chocolate. A hundred spectators were successively called up, each one performing an activity related to cooking, dictated by a screen, but yet containing an aspect of free will... every action could possibly contradict the previous one. Given the varying tastes and capabilities of those involved, the culinary result – to be ultimately shared as a collective meal – was appalling. Yet the spectacle of this gastronomic catastrophe, with its contrasts between individual taste and communal pressure, was delicious. The device, perhaps due to the fact that it was about food and it happened to be dinner-time, had a vested interest to encourage utterly incorrect attitudes amongst participants whom were asked to respect democracy.

Like other projects that were exclusively exhibited at Kortrijk (hence the practice of the Italian Anna Rispoli, moving from urban activism 'politics' to the creation of participatory works in public spaces), or which presented themselves solely as a space for formu-lating group reflection (The ArtsCommons), the above-mentioned projects all shared a more or less an avowed ideal: that of the common good, that participation, by virtue of its efforts to patch up the social fabric, could contribute to its restructuring. In this sense, the programme was meaningful both in terms of the approach taken by the Buda Arts Centre, which, while focused on its function as a laboratory and on being a producer, wants to question its role in the city, and with respect to the values promoted in Flanders, where over a quarter of a million children and young people participate in various youth movements on a weekly basis. As the 2.0 theatre piece *Web of Trust* (2016) presented by the Hungarian Edit Kaldor a week later in Brussels KunstenFestivaldesArts, the result of these collaborations is, ultimately, less important than the actual process by which participants become directly involved, satisfying their 'real interest in the other'– and their philanthropy. The fact that *Web of Trust*, which sets out to 'prepare for the revolution', fuelled by the discontent felt by widely differing groups of individuals, and their collaboration by means of a dedicated, if hardly resourceful, software, turns out to be theatrically mediocre, is of less impor-tance than what happens amongst the participants: the forging of a communal experience of revolutionary struggle, and even of the Paris Commune itself, this 'plot' that the Invisible Committee depicted in their political pamphlet *To Our Friends* (2014).

Political intelligence

As we have observed, this taste for participation may well have conflicting motives and applications between participation used as a scenic tool, particularly relevant when it comes to issues concerning different identities, and the idea of a joint project with a utilitarian purpose, satisfying the altruistic inclination we love to imagine we possess (and sometimes do). The participatory form can also at some point represent a deeply-felt need for the artist, in the sense it often is an excellent medium to share intimate experiences, a place where art's political function can vibrantly assert itself. Hence, participation becomes that tool of political understanding that may be discerned in the work of a Roger Bernat, or in that of Anne-Cécile Vandalem in her project *What can I do for you?* (2014-15) in Brussels, Liege, and Mons. Her work embodies a principle of urban-based works, questioning art's usefulness and usage, where the passer-by could be the sponsor. Public requests range from 'have the problems of child abuse heard by more than five hundred people,' to 'bring down the Belgian government'.

Participation can also be deployed by artists who are aware of the challenges of sharing their experiences in a given environment. Hence, the work (incidentally, highly contrasting) of the Egyptian Laila Soliman and the Lebanese Tania El Khoury. Both maintain a creative activity, or even are involved in activism, in their native countries, both partly educated in Europe, and also exhibit their projects elsewhere in the world. Yet, how is it possible to share the experience of war, of dictatorship, of repression, to a public in a peaceful democracy (or supposedly so) that has no experience of such woes? Both these artists could content themselves with just being a great playwright, or a charismatic performer. And yet, one of them has elected to relive the experience of the martyrs from Tahrir Square by having the audience read aloud calls demanding the trial of the Egyptian government for the death of the martyrs of the Egyptian Revolution (*No Time for Art o.o*, 2012), or by immersing the public in the bureaucratic nightmare of State Security Apparatus (*Here, There and Everywhere*, 2013). El Khoury imposes upon the spectator the destabilising role of a spy in the context of a civil war (*Jarideh*, 2010) or assigns them the role of an all-powerful male puppeteer manipulating from a distance a woman's body in public space (*Maybe If You Choreograph Me, You Will Feel Better*, 2011). Each time, these devices are means for the specta(c)tor to acquire a different political understanding of events, by means of a comparable experience generated by the performance.

Participate, as long as you can

If Paul Ardenne likened the development of participatory forms of visual arts from the 1990s to a disillusioned attempt to propose utopias, in an era that sanctions putting an end to ideologies, we cannot reduce the current trend to that demurral. The current revival of participatory art forms is unfolding *simultaneously* to social, community-based, activist or insurrectional approaches, which deploy similar devices (at times with the support of the engaged artists-activists in these circles) and serve, in turn, as a source of inspiration for artists. For better or worse, digital practices have trivialised the use of participation. Ultimately, the question becomes more complicated due to the fact that we have less and less of a sense of control over politics, on the one hand, and, on the other, the burgeoning deprivation of freedoms, (of expression, assembly, demonstration, opinion...), notably under the pretext of terrorism.

Confronted with governments who have forced us to swallow the fact (again, according to the Ulrich Beck's formulation in *Risk Society: Towards a New Modernity*, 1986) that they can do nothing for us, while actually take more account of the wishes of shareholders than the votes of the electorate, participating in a work of art might, perhaps, reassure us about our free will. Given the proliferation of draconian laws and the outright trampling of human rights, including those at our borders, participating offers us the illusion of living-together, where individual expression would be taken into account, where the other would not be deported. That theatre, from which the political world and its actors have so often borrowed its codes (and thanks to this relationship, remains the predestined locus for political questioning), has seen participatory devices multiply, should not astonish us. And while, faced with this trend, we certainly need to remain vigilant and critical of any ersatz form of democracy it generates, to dismiss them outright, as some elitist intellectuals have done, is an extremely arrogant position. For beyond its analgesic effect, participation in the arts has the merit of reminding us what it means to have an opinion and to directly engage, even should it be in a purely formal manner. A lesson that one day could prove quite useful, lest *they* ever want to impose that *we* no longer participate – except through obedience.

JUSTINE BOUTENS

EVERY ART PROPOSITION

CAN POTENTIALLY
BE EXPERIENCED
AS PARTICIPATORY

Participation is also a hot topic in Flanders. After the participation decree, a flanking policy stimulating participation in the domains of youth, arts, and sports, came into effect in 2008, the concept became a great deal more prominent. Its high point to date came in 2016, when it gained its own separate section on arts grant application forms.

But the question of what should be understood by the concept of participation remains with many organisations within the arts, as a recent survey by the magazine *Rekto:Verso* (no. 72, July 2016) reveals. According to the Flemish decree, it is about 'consolidating, increasing and widening participation' and the 'renewal and intensification of the participation of disadvantaged groups'. In concrete terms, this means reaching out to an existing audience more often and with a more diverse offering, tapping into a wider audience, and involving a fresh audience from disadvantaged groups.

This is a broad spectrum, ranging from art education to social-artistic work, with every possible variation in between. At CAMPO, we share the conviction that we need to play a role in a world that is facing huge challenges. We support artists who share this sense of urgency because we believe that art can have an impact. In our practice, we are generally confronted with four different rather traditional participatory theatre formats, which are always illustrated using an example of a creation that has previously been produced at CAMPO: an artistic collaboration with non-professional participants (e.g. *IN KOOR!* by Myriam Van Imschoot and Willem de Wolf from Cie. De Koe), in which older amateur actors are cast alongside drama students for a piece

Sarah Vanhee, *Lecture For Every One* (2013)

about choir rehearsals); group projects with non-professional participants (performances that work out a full trajectory for each venue with a group of local participants, such as *U Dikke Ma, een voetbalopera* by het KIP); performances with active audience interaction (the simplest form of audience participation), in which the theatre audience becomes part of the performance and/or makes a contribution to the piece, such as in *An Anthology of Optimism* by Pieter De Buysser and Jacob Wren, for which the audience could send in a suggestion that would be incorporated into the performance); and performances outside the theatre auditorium (site-specific projects whose goal is to reach an audience that would otherwise be unlikely to walk into an Arts Centre, such as *A-Tipis.* For this project (which was performed o.a. in Paris's Parc de la Villette), eight artists were asked to create an installation, and all of them were subsequently exhibited together in a public space).

Right from the early days of both Victoria and Nieuwpoorttheater, we have been producing and supporting projects that would now be labelled as participatory. Moreover, the focus on social topics, inclusion, and local anchoring has been there from the start. But setting up participatory projects is not always straightforward. Our constant search for new audiences is mostly a process of trial and error, without us sticking to particular methodologies or theoretical frameworks. Artistic performances are quite simply difficult to categorise. A key characteristic of CAMPO is that almost all projects, with the exception of *Buurtkeuken*, begin with an artistic interpretation. In this, we differ from what in Flanders is described as 'social-artistic work', whose starting point is people, and whose emphasis on the process and on guiding the participants is at least as important as the artistic outcome.

For this contribution, we will be focusing on three totally different cases. Whilst all are highly participatory, none of them can really be fitted into the rather traditional categories mentioned above. All three relate to our reply to the question of why participation is important, but all start from different premises. There is *Buurtkeuken*, a concept that unites the arts centre and local residents – two worlds that do not always meet; ONBETAALBAAR, a collective that brings together theatre makers, craftsmen, and their audience to re-evaluate an object or building; and Sarah Vanhee, whose performances include *Lecture For Every One*, in which she steps outside the theatre auditorium and encounters people unexpectedly.

The unusual thing about these projects is that they go one step further: they link social engagement (from social cohesion, to raising awareness about ecology, to caring for one another and the world) with the interpretation of participation that we are familiar with in Flanders, namely audience involvement.

Buurtkeuken (Neighbourhood Kitchen)

Since 2006, CAMPO has been organising a monthly *Buurtkeuken*. On the first Monday of the month, volunteers from the neighbourhood around CAMPO Nieuwpoort come together to cook. Cooking and eating together are the starting points here, with the goal being social cohesion. The (dozen or so) volunteers are assisted by a supervisor from CAMPO, who is always accompanied by a different professional chef, usually a restaurateur from the local area. By noon, the menu is presented to the volunteers, who together start cooking for around 120 people. There are also volunteers for the serving and the washing up, who are supplemented by CAMPO staff.

In the evening, the whole neighbourhood is welcome to come along, and everyone eats together on the theatre stage.

The key thing is that after the meal, there is always an artistic intervention, generally an insight into the working process of a theatre maker who is currently working at CAMPO. Thus local residents – who are often older people with no links to theatre or dance – gain an insight into what CAMPO is doing, there is greater involvement, and a number of people go on to find their way to our performances. In the meantime, many local residents have become generally interested in our work. Our ambition now is to attract a more diverse range of participants.

JUSTINE BOUTENS (JB) *How do you persuade people to come into a theatre auditorium for an evening meal?*

MANUEL HAEZEBROUCK (MH) We keep the thresholds very low. The price for the food is highly democratic, and we have a straightforward registration process which prioritises local residents. They are the first ones to get a flyer through their doors (plenty of people do not have computers), and it's only after the first round of registrations that we spread the invitation online.

The artistic interventions are also tailor-made for the local area: they are accessible and non-niche, or we simply take the work out of its niche for this particular occasion. For example, we have presented the work of Florentina Holzinger and Vincent Riebeek, with an act taken from the performance. Or we'll offer a debate: in December 2015, we staged the Zwartepieten debate [a discussion about whether in today's world it's appropriate to keep on using the traditional 'Black Pete' figures in December's St. Nicholas celebrations] which was raging in Flanders at the time, at the theatre, and tried to open up the discussion.

JB *What challenges do you face?*

MH The fact that preparations take place during the day on a Monday inevitably results in a rather homogenous group of volunteers, which is mostly comprised of pensioners. In an ideal situation, this team would be a mixture of ages and backgrounds. We are currently working to address this challenge.

Onbetaalbaar (Priceless)
ONBETAALBAAR is a creative collective that has been working since 2012 towards 'materialism with emotion', based on its love of objects. It is both a workplace and a think tank, a place

Atelier ONBETAALBAAR

in which furniture makers, upholsterers, writers, philosophers, DIY enthusiasts, product designers, restaurateurs, and graphic artists – in short, workers and thinkers – come together to study the value of, the problems with and the potential of recovered materials, and the stories that go with them.

In 2017, the collective will be moving into CAMPO boma, CAMPO's studio, which is located in an area with a high concentration of migrants in the nineteenth century belt around Ghent. Its long-term residence will ensure that there is continuous activity over the coming years, with the residencies of theatre makers, artists, collectives, and thinkers from a diverse range of disciplines. The audience and local residents are welcome to come in and take a look: the doors will regularly be thrown open for events such as lectures, exhibitions, workshops, and a weekly open studio for interested parties with varying degrees of experience.

ONETAALBAAR is a story of co-creation between workers and thinkers. It will be touring Flanders with projects such as *Veiling der Dingen, Oplichten, KRAAK,* and *Regie der Gebouwen.*

Interview with Sophie De Somere, one of the driving forces behind the project

JB *How did ONBETAALBAAR come about?*

SOPHIE DE SOMERE (SDS) ONBETAALBAAR grew out of the understanding that a large number of people collect things with the intention of 'doing something with them at a later date'. All kinds of circumstances then intervene to thwart their plans, but they are unable to throw things away because of the personal stories behind them. For instance, something might be an heirloom or a flea market find, or have been intended for a project that has been postponed. We wanted to offer a solution to this problem by working with these items and breathing new life into them.

At the same time, Elsemieke Scholte from detheatermaker was running a project about writers and theatre makers who work all day long, but who are sometimes left with just a single sentence at the end of the day. Her aim was to devise a preparatory process for theatre that would culminate in a tangible result; like the work of a furniture maker, for example. This was the theme for the first *Veiling der Dingen* [*Auction of Things*]: the items were all brought together for an auction, an encounter between slow and fast-paced work where writers and theatre makers could recount the stories behind the objects.

JB *How do you set to work?*

SDS ONBETAALBAAR involves working with people and objects. We try to encourage people to see what they can find in their attic basement, garage, etc. The state that the materials are in is less important than the personal stories behind them. This is the key thing for us.

For the *Veiling der Dingen*, for example, a process that begins with the idea of breathing new life into unwanted objects and culminates in a public auction, we publicise a series of local open days in every city, where people can bring objects in. The objects serve as a means of introduction: they are the beginning of the story. They help us to break the ice with the donors, so that we can subsequently talk to them and determine what to do with the objects.

The objects are an opportunity for us to look inside one another. The donors have the opportunity to see our project and our workshop, and in turn we learn something about the world in which they live. The fact that we will be breathing new life into the objects also provides a reason for them to come back, and for us to build up a relationship with them.

In parallel to the contribution made by the furniture makers, designers, etc., the theatre makers and writers start to create the passports and catalogues for the auctions. With the catalogue and the auction book, you can also take the stories of the objects home with you, whether you have purchased an item or not. We thus share the stories, not just the objects.

JB   *Do you work with specific target groups?*

SDS   We travel from city to city, collaborating with each to understand where the opportunities lie, and exactly which target groups they wish to appeal to. In Brussels, for example, we worked on the theme of employment, running projects with people experiencing psychological problems, bike repair shops, etc. For the *Veiling der Kinderen* [*Children's Auction*] in Ghent, we collaborated with MUS-E in a number of schools with children from a variety of different ethnic cultural background. For them/ their parents, there is often a taboo surrounding second-hand items. Our goal is to diminish the taboo by working with the children on the concept of upcycling.

A project such as *Roestvrij* [*Rust-free*], which we started up in Ostend in 2016, was based on a newspaper article about senior citizens living on the coast. A large number of people choose to retire to the seaside, but become isolated because the city and the housing have not been adjusted to meet their needs. This is something that we will be working on in 2016-17.

The story of the city is also important to us. We are always looking for a characteristic aspect of a city or an interesting way to approach it. For example, Mechelen used to be a leading furniture city, until the factories had to reorient themselves in response to the changed social and economic context. We discovered a whole arsenal of furniture into which we were able to breathe new life.

JB *Your projects are certainly about engagement, but this is done subtly; never in a patronising way and mostly tongue-in-cheek.*

SDS It would be wrong to try and raise people's awareness through finger wagging; instead you need to convince people with your passion and engagement. In *Oplichten* [*Scamming*], in which we organise one-on-one bidding in dialogue with one of our makers, we are not going to patronisingly accuse anyone of offering Bangladesh-style prices. But in the meantime, we do ensure that we are creating awareness of the fact that the profit margins should be directed to the right people, in the hope that in a few years' time this becomes self-evident.

    Regie der Gebouwen [*Buildings Agency*], also has an injustice as its starting point. When a public building is completed, it is normally only the mayor and a few dignitaries who cut the ribbons, at a ceremony with canapés and drinks. We want to celebrate the completion of a new building with its makers, the people who have worked on the building site, and their stories: from the bricklayers and the plumbers to the carpenters and the wallpaper designers. Together with Barbara Raes from Beyond the Spoken, we give the people who have worked on the building the chance to say goodbye with a ceremony, so that they can be involved in the transitory phase and be part of the finalising of the project, after which they can all hand it over to the public together.

    With *KRAAK* [*SQUAT*], we take the time to say goodbye to a building before it is demolished. For example, in a cultural centre's music school, we gathered together the stories of the music teachers and the diction class and shared them with visitors one last time by immortalising them on the walls prior to the latter's demolition.

JB *What barriers do you face?*

SDS Due to a lack of time and resources, or because of the need to make compromises, we sometimes have to water down the design that we had worked out in advance. But we are a collective, and therefore want to keep on deciding as much as possible as a team. Moreover, we often have to disappoint people who want to lend a hand in the run-up to an auction, as we don't have the material or the time for this. But offering everyone the opportunity to contribute to the ONBETAALBAAR community is a future dream that we can address in the form of an open studio.

Lecture For Every One – Sarah Vanhee

Sarah Vanhee's artistic practice is linked to performance, visual art, and literature. It uses different formats and is often (re) created in situ, all over Europe. Her trajectory at CAMPO started off in 2009, and has continued up to now, touring with *Oblivion* (2015). From her extensive biography, we highlight some of the projects she has created that have taken a particular participatory approach: *Untitled* (2012), consisting of a series of individual visits to private houses where people talk about the artworks they have at home, thus providing a counterweight to the definitions of art as viewed by professional curators and the art scene. *Lecture For Every One* (2013), a series of unannounced artistic interventions in different places where people gather together for a specific purpose, either private or professional. *Lecture For Every One* is a short lecture on contemporary society as a co-creation by everyone, ranging from banks to football teams and city councils. Most recently, *Absent Images* (2016) is disseminated via public canvasses in the city and throughout the country. Billboard panels, advertising spaces, empty walls, or windows all become carriers of a political message, a written apology to the refugees, in eight languages.

Sarah Vanhee is a co-founder and member of Manyone.

JB *What does participation mean to you?*

SARAH VANHEE (SV) I do not have a personal take on the concept of participation in art. Within the arts, 'participation' is largely an agenda imposed from above, by the happy few in the art world as we know it: white, highly educated and overwhelmingly male. It is intolerable that these happy few should control what art is, how it should be used, and who should participate in it.

Another problem is that participation is often measured on the basis of a certain degree of active participation, but that too is relative: a regular spectator in the auditorium can be more involved in a performance than someone who is physically taking part in it. Every art proposition can potentially be experienced as participative.

71

JB *With* Untitled *you showed the audience people in their own homes and allowed them to explain what art means to them. As a concept, this fits effortlessly into the participative picture, but in an interview, you distance yourself from this: 'My work is sometimes mistaken for the socially engaged art that aims for social inclusion or representation. This is never my goal per se. In the case of* Untitled, *I would work with anyone who would answer my question: "What is art at your place, and can we have a conversation about that?" The diversity of answers came with the diversity of people – the outcome of an open question, not of a strategic plan.'*

SV Identity is a complex concept that cannot be reduced to statistics. For *Untitled* I worked with a 'diverse' group of people, but behind this selection lay a discussion between a number of singular individuals. The diversity came about through dialogue and exchange, not through a formal compliance with statistics.

What's also important to me as an artist is that I don't have to sign up to a social agenda, as is often the case in the UK. I am not required to deliver results, bring about improvement, as would be expected in prisons or in drama therapy. As the art has no 'purpose' it cannot be instrumentalised.

Moreover, it is important to understand that a white elite currently determines how art is defined. I don't see why people should be obliged to be involved at any cost. In my opinion, this is an abuse of both the art and the people. But that doesn't mean that there is no legitimate desire to discuss what form art should take in today's society; indeed the opposite is true.

JB *But you specifically connect to others; your audience is very closely involved in* Lecture For Every One, *for example.*

SV I choose not to see *Lecture For Every One* as a participatory project, as I would otherwise have to make compromises. That's why it's also more of an 'intrusion' than an invitation to participate.

I want to do projects like *Lecture For Every One* as a human being. I do not believe that discussions about politics and society can be usefully held in an environment full of like-minded people. This achieves nothing. That's why I'm so interested in a society that makes discussion possible, but which is not apolitical.

After all the projects that had taken place outside the art institute, I had a strong desire to go back into the auditorium, but now there is also *Absent Images*, a project that I do not regard as an artwork of mine, but as one that I am implementing as a citizen. The huge advantage of art in society is what, in the tradition of Diogenes, they describe as *Parrhesia*, or the fool, the joker. As an artist, you can be a free spirit, because people know that you sometimes do strange things, and they accept that. You have that safe haven, and I conveniently make use of it.

JB   *To date,* Lecture For Every One *has interrupted over 300 meetings, a.o. in Brussels, Stockholm, Berlin, Paris, and Athens. How does this work, exactly?*

SV   For *Lecture For Every One* I actually choose to invert the concept of the audience. In normal circumstances, an audience decides whether or not to go to a performance, or which performance it wants to see. Now I decide myself which audience I want to appeal to: young or old, left or right wing, NGO or business, SME or multinational, political or apolitical, a particular religion or cultural background, etc. Within this, my preference is for those who will potentially be the least receptive to my words.

Together with the arts institute that is organising the lectures, we draw up a list of possible places where we would like to stage them, and then try to find a way in through a contact person. Once this has been achieved, there is always one person from within the organisation, company, etc. who is abreast of the situation, and who lets us in during the meeting. I come in, am briefly introduced by the company's contact person and I then deliver the lecture, which takes 15 minutes. The tone is one of a 'private chat'. If any questions are asked during the lecture, I answer them, and this might lead to a lengthy discussion. When the lecture is finished, I leave. Afterwards, we contact the organisation to offer them the opportunity to give feedback. People can also react via online fora.

JB   *How did people who had become an audience against their will react to* Lecture For Every One*?*

SV   *Lecture For Every One* unlocked more than I had hoped it would, and this was also the case in the art institutes. I received confirmation of a tendency that I am seeing everywhere. Whatever the context, once we had made it in there – as preparing for the lectures was no mean feat – it was rarely a

73

negative experience. Beforehand, I had thought that I would be trotting out too many self-evident points (e.g. Vanhee presents an analysis of a neoliberal society, and talks about care, love, etc.). But in the event, many people admitted that these were not topics to which they had given any thought, due to the pressures of maintaining both a family and a career. They literally said that they never took the time or physically had the time to 'stop and think about these things'. This too is shocking.

The most striking thing for me was that the proposal was the least well received within the arts world. There is a striking lack of collectivism, which arises from the fear of losing individuality or singularity, whilst people in other contexts perhaps have less of a problem with this.

JB Oblivion *was the first performance that you have created for a theatre auditorium for a long time, alone, with only your rubbish from the past year. Will you be moving away from the auditorium again for your next project?*

SV I am currently making a film in a prison. After that, I will be creating another auditorium production. And for *Public Learning* I will be working in the public space again with a wide range of people. Learning, or the oral transfer of knowledge, will be playing a central role in this project. We have all had a teacher, a mother, a grandmother who has taught us different kinds of knowledge and wisdom. I am fascinated by this embodied knowledge, this oral tradition, and by how it is transferred.

The idea for this new project flows from the experience of being gripped by knowledge, of being truly inspired by someone. The transfer of knowledge often takes place within a closed, institutional domain, with little in the public domain. I would like this transfer to take place in a public space. So once again, I will be focusing on a gathering, like with *Lecture For Every One*, but this time the purpose will be to learn.

CAMPO (box)

The Ghent-based but internationally oriented arts centre CAMPO could be seen as a toolbox for artists, and a house that covers the whole spectrum of performing arts: research and development, production, touring, and presentation. It responds to artistic proposals and artists and challenges them with specific assignments. It does this both in one-off joint ventures (such as with Tim Etchells, Gob Squad, Philippe Quesne, and Milo Rau) but these can also be the start of a long-term trajectory (as with Pieter Ampe, Sarah Vanhee, Florentina Holzinger, or, more recently, Robbert&Frank Frank&Robbert and Louis Vanhaverbeke). Apart from creating its own productions (many of them with international co-producers), CAMPO also offers support for the work of kindred artists and companies, and its studios are regularly opened up to an endless series of homeless artists. Ever since CAMPO started as an arts centre, it has been addressing new audiences and communities (with a particular focus on young people) through participation projects, student festivals (e.g. *Mayday Mayday*), a monthly *Neighbourhood Kitchen*, debates on arts and politics, and more. On top of that, CAMPO is also a place for the presentation of performance, theatre, dance, and cross-overs from Belgium and abroad.

CAMPO was founded in January 2008 out of a fusion of Victoria and Nieuwpoorttheater. The substantive legacy and artistic expertise of the former Victoria (an international production platform that produced works by, among others, Alain Platel, Jérôme Bel, Josse De Pauw, and Tim Etchells) and Nieuwpoorttheater (a presentation house focusing on fundamental research into the relationship between art, community, cultural identity, popular culture, power, and the social context) provided the basis for CAMPO's artistic plan. This arts centre has three sites in Ghent where it can create and present work.

CITYTALK

ELENA BASTERI (EB) *You have been head of the Bürgerbühne in Dresden since it was founded seven years ago. Could you introduce yourself by telling us a bit about your background and how you became head of the Bürgerbühne?*

MIRIAM TSCHOLL (MT) I grew up in a rural area where there wasn't much in the way of culture. A municipal theatre was a real object of desire for me, and I longed to have access to that type of institution.

I went on to study Cultural Sciences and Aesthetic Practice at the University of Hildesheim, where I opted to specialise in theatre. The programme takes an interdisciplinary approach and uses a blend of theory and practice to continuously identify and explore new paths. The boundaries between social action and theatre are also a subject of constant focus and reflection. I stayed on after graduation to teach theatre, and was also the founding director of an independent theatre group. We tried out a variety of constellations involving us, professional actors, and amateurs performing together on stage. It was after a youth theatre project at Schauspiel Hannover that the creative director asked me if I'd like to come with him to Dresden and head up a new department for professional theatre with non-professional actors. And so the Bürgerbühne was born.

EB *Perhaps it would be sensible to give readers who don't speak German an explanation of the term 'Bürger'. What exactly does it mean, and does the Bürgerbühne use it in a particular way?*

DYNAAAMO! (2015)

MT   'Bürger' is a fuzzy term. In the constitutional sense it means a citizen of a city or country, yet in the broader sense it means anyone who does not hold political office. At the Bürgerbühne we use the term inclusively – when we say 'Bürger', we mean everyone. This is important when advertising for participants, for example citizens who have had to flee from something at some point in their life. We try to break down the term using combinations such as the 'Homosexual Citizen's Club' or the 'Club for Citizens with Special Talents'. This enables us to be specific but still cast the net wide. Whenever we address the citizens of Dresden, we are addressing society in its heterogeneous entirety. We aim to communicate with all generations, all social backgrounds, and of course citizens of all origins. Our stages have been graced by punks, bankers, followers of Judaism and Islam, midwives, undertakers, fans of the Dynamo Dresden football team, men in the midst of a midlife crisis, and many more besides. We attempt to avoid strict classifications and instead define new groups when addressing potential participants. One example might be to look for a group of citizens who have too much free time on their hands, which could draw responses from the unemployed, pensioners, bored teachers, and housewives alike.

EB *It must be particularly challenging to engage citizens in cultural projects in a place like Dresden, a city where citizens have taken such extreme, polar stances in the public sphere. As a citizen of Dresden, could you give us a brief insight into the current socio-political landscape in the city?*

MT Dresden is complicated. I suppose you need to view the city against the backdrop of its past if you really want to understand it. The date it all tends to come back to is 13 February 1945, when Dresden was bombed particularly mercilessly by the Allies. Unlike in other cities, Dresden's enduring myth of victimization has prevented the proper digestion of German war guilt. This is compounded by the reluctance of the GDR to properly reappraise the National Socialist era. The GDR's policy of isolation and the lack of contact between its population and foreigners also remain a source of xenophobic tendencies. The government of the GDR not only suppressed contact between its citizens and guest workers from other socialist states, but also denied the existence of extreme right-wing movements. The CDU has unfortunately continued in the same vein since reunification.

Many people benefitted from reunification, but there were also those who didn't. The collapse and subsequent reappraisal of the GDR is also likely to have destroyed trust in systems, politicians and the elite in general. With this in mind, it is worth noting that the global crisis of confidence in financial capitalism is particularly frightening for those living in areas which have already witnessed plenty of crises and upheaval. All of this combines with a strange pride in being a 'true' Saxon and a government which was long reluctant to even acknowledge problems – let alone deal with them – to prepare what is clearly fertile ground for xenophobic thought and action. Right now we are unfortunately experiencing a noticeable spike in both. The situation is even worse than it was a few years ago, when we as a theatre had already long identified the issues and begun integrating them into our creative output.

EB *You describe the Bürgerbühne as a model which functions according to a particular set of rules and working methods. How does the model work?*

MT The Bürgerbühne is a department of the Staatsschauspiel theatre in Dresden. We enable the citizens of Dresden and the surrounding region to take to the stage as part of five repertory productions per season as well as a large number of theatre clubs with a more pedagogical focus.

The productions are put together professionally by a director and a team of specialists. They have all the theatre's resources at their disposal – from scriptwriting support, technical equipment, props, costumes, and make-up to the use of the theatre's rehearsal spaces and dress rehearsals on the actual stage. In that sense they are identical to any of the theatre's other productions.

In the early stages of a production, we carefully determine which topic is relevant to the city and which citizens we want to give a platform to. We are especially keen to welcome as broad a cross-section of the population as possible onto the stage. To give an example, the Dynamo Dresden football fans whose production premiered last season were followed into our repertoire by an ensemble of citizens who speak Arabic. You see, Dynamo is known for being tainted by xenophobia, and we wanted to build bridges by first telling one story and then the other. The Bürgerbühne always aims to be a place where lots of different people can tell their diverse stories in a huge variety of ways. In some cases we draw on classical source texts, in others we opt for a sober documentary style, musical theatre, or comedy. Whatever the format, our directors look for methods and means of expression which cannot simply be adopted from professional theatre with professional actors. There are two key questions during the conceptualization phase: Why does the material need to be brought to the stage by non-professional actors, and what skills do they bring with them that a professional ensemble would lack? If we fail to answer those questions and the audience leaves thinking 'Not bad for a bunch of amateurs, but I'd rather have seen it performed by professionals' then we've failed to achieve our goals.

Each production is performed on one of three stages at the Kleines Haus [the Staatsschauspiel's second venue] and may remain in our repertoire for anywhere between 12 and 40 performances.

Our clubs, on the other hand, present the results of their workshops a maximum of three times. Each club is led by one or more of our specialists in theatre pedagogy, actors, or assistant directors. The clubs are extremely popular – not only because rehearsals are less intensive, but also because there is no selection

Mischpoke (2015)

process and participants are welcome to come back and join
another club next time round. Demand for places goes up every
year, and we now offer around 13 clubs per intake. That means
that roughly 400 of Dresden's citizens take to the stage as part
of our productions and clubs each season. There are nevertheless
far more applicants than there are places – we receive anywhere
between 20 and 250 applications depending on the criteria
defined for the club or production in question. Acting talent is
rarely a requirement, and it is usually citizen's biographies and
willingness to talk about them that counts. This is especially true
during the intensive selection workshops carried out prior to
productions.

EB   *A model with strict rules has an important part to play in
ensuring that the complex development of a theatrical production
runs as smoothly as possible. But working with amateurs and their
biographies – be they young, migrants, unemployed, hooligans,
or men in the midst of a midlife crisis – must be associated with
a lot of emotionality, fragility, and in particular unforeseen
circumstances. How does the Bürgerbühne model allow for and
protect these emotional, uncontrollable elements?*

Meeting at Monday Café

MT   There is indeed a difference between a Bürgerbühne
production and working with an ensemble of salaried
professional actors in this regard. One distinct advantage is that
the date of the premiere is set in stone. It's amazing, but over
the last seven years every premiere has taken place on schedule.
And despite any crises or difficulties during rehearsals, both
performers and teams have always been happy with what they've
achieved. Most productions go remarkably smoothly and all
performers remain committed and motivated. I mean, they should
do, they've volunteered to take part! We emphasise the fact that
theatre is not therapy, and if we notice any signs of psychological
instability in a candidate we will generally turn them down.

This notwithstanding, there are also productions where we
consciously push ourselves to the limits and the director and their
assistant in particular really have their work cut out organising
rehearsals and keeping the production together. This requires a
high level of social and emotional commitment.

One example is *Meine Akte und ich* (2013), a production
which saw victims of the Stasi stand side-by-side with former
Stasi employees on stage. It was emotional dynamite during

rehearsals! The thing is that the director, Clemens Bechtel, possessed the social and communicative skills required in order to not only help the group navigate some difficult emotional processes, but also mediate between performers. The directors selected for Bürgerbühne productions therefore all have excellent soft skills. As I see it, this is one area where Bürgerbühne differs from theatre with professional actors, where the skills I've just mentioned are not necessarily compulsory but certainly an advantage.

From a personal perspective, my most difficult production to date was *Morgenland* (2015), which premiered with its ensemble of Arabic-speaking citizens in the 2015-16 season. In addition to language-related communication problems, as a director I was also faced with tasks that stretched both my skills and my strength to the limit. Seven out of the 11 performers were refugees, and their precarious social situation meant that they had to take care of existential matters such as official appointments, accommodation, and their education before they could commit to the production. The translator who came to rehearsals was the only one they had access to, so it was only natural that they often used rehearsals to talk to him about existential issues. As we were in many cases the only Germans our performers had any contact with, it was clearly impossible to break off the relationships that are a prerequisite for a successful premiere as soon as rehearsals finished. Some of the younger performers still call me 'Mama Miriam' – a year on from our premiere. This type of responsibility makes what is already a very demanding workload even more challenging. One solution might be to cooperate with a social worker, yet that would only make sense if the theatre created a position for them and funded them throughout the duration of the production.

The Club for Citizens with Special Talents is another example of our work. In this case, the club is run by two specialists in theatre pedagogy and all its members are mentally handicapped. Here again, we have chosen to work with this group on a continuous basis as a result of the social and organisational challenges involved. It is also worth noting that the team which supports the Club for Citizens with Special Talents is much larger than usual and benefits from additional funding.

The bottom line is that professional theatre with non-professional performers requires directors and their teams to not only possess excellent social skills, but also be prepared for the fact that productions involving more difficult target groups may require a different approach. Theatres and their staff need to be able to react with flexibility. Just because even large organisations characterised by clear procedures and structures are able to do so does not necessarily make it easy. I therefore see room for further analysis and development in this area.

EB *Performers are generally only permitted to take part in one Bürgerbühne production, the aim being to avoid the risk of establishing a second permanent ensemble at the theatre. On the one hand that seems a logical move, yet on the other it seems to contradict the notion of sustainable, long-term participation...*

MT Both approaches have their advantages and their disadvantages. I tend towards openness and the wealth of opportunities that come with it. Participation does not end as soon as the applause dies down at the end of a premiere. A production might remain in our repertoire for up to three seasons, and during that time its ensemble remains in close contact with us. Even after the curtain goes down on their final performance, we often see each other at various events in and around the theatre. And they can always decide to join one of our clubs.

EB *What audience does the Bürgerbühne cater to? Does it target a particular niche, or is the aim to encourage the Staatsschauspiel's traditional audience to switch between productions performed by professionals and the Bürgerbühne? Performers' relatives and friends have a natural interest in coming to see them, but why would other theatregoers choose to watch a play performed by amateur actors?*

MT We haven't carried out any definitive audience analysis. A non-representative survey nevertheless found that each performer attracts an average of around 25 friends and relatives to at least one performance of their production. But it must be said that productions can vary hugely in terms of their success. In our experience, the audience's decision is highly dependent on the relevance of the topic to them. We've also noticed that they relate to Bürgerbühne performers to an above-average degree.

EB   *Dresden's Bürgerbühne is the first of its kind and has established itself as a trendsetter. There are now 19 other 'Bürgerbühnes' in Germany, an international network has also taken shape. Is there regular exchange and cooperation, and what form does it take?*

MT   That's nearly right! There aren't 19 other 'Bürgerbühnes' per se, but a workshop on the concept of Bürgerbühne was attended by representatives from 19 German theatres which have developed a Bürgerbühne or a similar model over the last few years. There have already been three Bürgerbühne conferences in Dresden, Mannheim, and Karlsruhe, as well as two international Bürgerbühne festivals in Dresden and Mannheim. The third Bürgerbühnenfestival will be hosted by Theater Freiburg in 2017. We aim to continue strengthening cooperation at both national and international level.

EB   *The Bürgerbühne was founded as part of a drive by the Staatsschauspiel's Creative Director, Wilfried Schulz, to attract more people into the theatre. It can therefore be classified as an audience development strategy. At the same time, the Bürgerbühne makes a huge social contribution by bringing people together to enjoy a unique, joint experience among a constellation of people which would otherwise never have met. To a certain extent you kill two birds with one stone, and the model appears to combine both brilliance and efficiency. Do you have any self-criticisms, are there any points of friction or aspects you are not satisfied with and wish to improve?*

MT   I see a number of artistic, social, and political reasons to value the work of the Bürgerbühne.
   If I had to pick out a difficulty, it would probably be interaction between the theatre's scriptwriting team and the Bürgerbühne. In Dresden they are two separate departments who work together on a sporadic basis. Cooperation on scriptwriting is currently unsatisfactory for both parties due to the fact that Bürgerbühne productions are accompanied by not only a far greater scriptwriting workload, but also far more organisational and social investment than is required when working with professional actors. Theater Freiburg has adopted an interesting approach which sees scriptwriters also take on responsibility for organisational and social tasks. As far as

I know, the theatre has even made interest and experience in working with non-professional performers a prerequisite for new scriptwriters. It is nevertheless worth noting that Freiburg do much less work of this type than us, and that specialisation and a dedicated management team – the Dresden model – also has its advantages. One issue I'm really not sure about is whether or not Bürgerbühne employees can be expected to maintain such a high level of social responsibility year after year. There is a huge amount of communication and mediation involved. The strain needs to be reduced by incorporating more social workers and specialists in theatre pedagogy who see such tasks as their sole responsibility and do not have the additional burden of leading or organising their own projects.

EB   *We've spoken about the 'Monday Café', a new format created by the Bürgerbühne as a direct reaction to current events in Dresden. I'm fascinated by the influence political and social life in a city can have on its theatres, and it seems fitting that a theatre created for and driven by a city's citizens should act as an antenna which both detects and facilitates reaction to urgent social issues.*
      How did you hit on the idea of the Monday Café?

MT   Our Creative Director, Wilfried Schulz, called me up during the summer break. Homes for refugees were being boycotted; scabies had broken out in temporary tent camps. We said 'We've got to do something. And this time it can't be theatre'. After getting in touch with the Red Cross, the Ausländerrat [an advocacy group for foreign nationals] and a number of volunteers, I came to the conclusion that there was nowhere for the citizens of Dresden and refugees to engage in exchange. Seeing as we have both plenty of space and good ties with the local population, I set up the Monday Café as a meeting place for refugees and the citizens of Dresden. We now essentially empty the Kleines Haus between 3pm and 11pm every Monday and welcome around 150 refugees and citizens for a chat, workshops, informative talks, parties, or discussions on important issues.

      We've reacted to what is a difficult humanitarian situation, to a certain extent we've been forced to do so as a result of political failures. The project presents us with an entirely new challenge, and a substantial one at that. We are currently in talks with political representatives about our continued ability to finance it – and for how long.

ROGER BERNAT & ROBERTO FRATINI SERAFIDE

SEEING
ONESELF
LIVING

It was a large room. Full of people. All kinds. And they had all arrived at the same building at more or less the same time. And they were all free. And they were all asking themselves the same question: What is behind that curtain?

Laurie Anderson, *Born, never asked* (1982)

Any culture is *service*. [...] There is no domination without service in this world; human beings submit themselves voluntarily, and those who believe to exert their domination in freedom and at their will are more subjugated than anybody else.

Johan Huizinga, *The Playful and the Serious* (2014)

Once the singularity of theatre has faded away, multiplied and liquidated on countless screens and platforms; once the theatrical apparatus has ceased to be the mechanism by which the political game becomes an object (or a subject); once the characters have ceased to embody any sort of ethical or psychological model – theatre has completed its dematerialisation; it has become once and for all just another mechanism among those deployed by post-modernism in order to rebuild a social body once destroyed. Setting aside the significant therapeutic rage performed by cultural policies ensuring its (conservational, preconceived, uplifting) 'legitimacy', theatre lacks currently, more than ever before, any political and cultural legitimation.

And yet, released by the mechanisms that have been taking its place since the mid-nineteenth century, theatre becomes, as pointed out by Pedro G. Romero in the essay 'Actors, Situations,

Outcomes: Theater Machine and Theater: Subaltern Stages in the Spanish State' (2007), 'a preferred instrument for political, cultural and philological analysis of the social body'. The stage box bursts as a place of representation, and it is the social body as a whole that becomes theatrical. It is precisely when theatre loses the position it used to have that it takes the responsibility of elaborating a critique of the mechanisms that are now, once democracy has become a global form of government, in charge of representing reality with purely theatrical technologies.

Since the early days of modern times, the world has been shaped through mechanisms that, following disciplinary or surveillance strategies, have been changing the stage of human relations. Ezra Park summarised it in the early twentieth century, asserting that the crowds had become an audience. Subject to their workplace in a factory, the desk in a classroom or the seat in a cinema, human beings incorporate an ability to pay attention and listen that makes them an admirable spectator. This has led to the point that the refinement of mechanisms in the last decades, becoming more digital and lighter than ever before, allows for mobilisation and interactivity in a sort of emancipation through movement, which has taken the audiences away from theatre, yet at the cost of having them carry it along.

Citizens have become the audience of a fiction without actors. The spectators look at each other astonished, expecting that somebody takes the initiative and stands up as an actor. The scenery surrounding them is without any doubt a stage design. They take out their pocket devices to take a picture of the set. First they intend to push aside other spectators who take the landscape like intruders. Yet they quickly understand that there are no other actors than themselves, the drama will not have the panache they had dreamt of and the picture will not shine as it used to. In a drama without actors, the audience feels constrained to take part.

Long before climbing on this stage, the Cartesian doubt had dragged citizens away from the scenery they were intimately united with. Now, being on the stage of modern times, they not only become aware of their condition as characters, but also notice that they are part of a group participating in a drama without knowing its script. They fear being manipulated, excluded and repressed, and hence multiply those mechanisms that, as Giorgio Agamben points out in his article 'Une métaphysique critique pourrait naître comme science des dispositifs...' ['A Critical Metaphysics Could Be Born as a Science of Apparatuses'], (2001), 'do not work by separating large confuse crowds, but by spreading differential individualities'. Such devices and mechanisms *liberate* them by *submitting* them to a fake emancipation that is the more integral as it is based on the myth of constantly increasing connectivity (between machines and terminals, of course). The fictional performance of such citizen-actors is however anything but an act of *interpretation*. The positivity of power traded in the (non-)ideologies of 'positive thinking' consists precisely of deleting any interval, blank space, and room for disconnection that may expose the overall script to the risk of being interpreted and not just *executed*. Everything shall occur on a stage from now on, and hence following the rules of theatre, which endure in the memories of the characters in a more or less remote way.

When citizens become spectators, they feel the need to act. This paradox described by Georges Balandier in *El poder en escenas* [*Power Scenes*], (1994) with many examples taken from Africanist political anthropology becomes widespread in democracies pretending to have people's sovereignty. 'Power separates, isolates, makes sick; this is known to everybody. Above all, it changes those who gain it', and those gaining power become at the same time spectators of the community enthroning them and feel free to act upon it, changing its destiny. The current political and economic regime makes citizens sovereign, thus turning them simultaneously into spectators and actors – *spect-actors*, to put it in Boal's words.

So which is the place of theatre as an artistic practice, at a point at which reality is manifested as theatre and citizens are encouraged to be actors and spectators at the same time? What properties has a theatre that does not distinguish between stage and audience, between actor and spectator anymore? It is under such circumstances that it is worth pointing out the singularity of theatre as a collective project: in Darko Suvin's words, an 'experimental space and laboratory of the collective'. From its non-place, theatre operates like a cruel, emancipating machine in which, like the mechanisms of our century, the *mot d'ordre* is to participate. If theatre is a critical rethinking of reality, a reality shaped according to the dogma of participation, it will yearn for being rethought by theatrical mechanisms that set up participation in the least dogmatic, most dialectic, and even most critical way possible. Hence it is not only about working out a critique of the mechanisms, but theatre will also inevitably be a critique of the community as *work in progress* and *unfinished fiction*.

Theatre has historically refrained from participating in many varied ways. In this respect, it is inconsistent from a theoretical point of view to pretend to articulate the defence of theatrical participatory mechanisms by presenting them as the *dernier cri* of poetics. Likewise, it would be irresponsible to claim theatre as a place where the aspirations of any community are projected. The difference, if any, will lie in that the perspective of participatory theatre has never before had such a favourable background. Hence the need for unfolding the dialectical stealth, being cunning and, if necessary, cruel; and for considering that if democracy pretends to be *given* beforehand anywhere, theatre is the most appropriate place for undermining the guarantee of it being *actually* given, in order to blow up the sensationalist *illusion* that fighting for it is not appropriate anymore. All in all, theatre is the most suitable circumstance to renegotiate the fictional statuses hiding behind any democratic evidence. If participation irradiates to all areas of praxis by means of a sort of *thaumaturgy* (prodigy and healing), it will be necessary and urgent to irradiate afterwards to all areas of *theoresis* and *poiesis* by means of a sort of *dramaturgy* (doubt, diagnose, and detour).

Within the theatrical framework, extending the startling credibility the cultural discourse usually gives to participation as an absolute value and a miraculous *app* means to ignore that participation is not new (it is very old indeed) and that it is precisely its performative applications and updates that have been both emancipatory and regressive. We must not forget that theatre as a mechanism for mobilisation has been very often involved in processes in which the collectivisation of emotions has led whole societies to dreadful adventures. The sensual can be easily used as consensual. And the regressive only exposes the audience to the same temptation that makes that savoury blackmailing, the 'mandatory temptation' to be children propelled again and again by the civilisation of consumption as a whole.

From both an aesthetic and a political point of view, the dichotomy between a mechanism of *participation* as a promise of emancipation and a *traditional* mechanism as a guarantee of oppression is wrong. Being unable to avoid it, theatre needs to accept to reconstruct and revalorise the radical and etymological kinship between the ideas of *theatre* and *theory*, both set up not in the register of *experience* but in that of *vision*. Theatre will have theoretical power if it is able to reconstruct the potential of vision of each spectator through the mere discrepancy between *experience* as a possibility and *action* as a reality. 'Seeing oneself living' is a radically theatrical experience because it is never a comforting one.

Roger Bernat, *Displacement of La Moneda Palace* (2014)

Its prime effect is, first and foremost, to demolish our self-assertion of being good interpreters of ourselves. An ultimate metamorphosis of the Brechtian interpreter (especially if thinking of Brecht's didactic dramas), the spectator of a participatory mechanism is taken to state, among other things, that the spectator role is a fiction that becomes poetically and politically prolific as soon as it is accepted as fiction. The participatory mechanism turns out to be poetically effective when the convincement of being a good actor creates unexpectedly inconsistent or ridiculous effects.

Seen from this perspective, participation provides neither the holistic benefits of experiencing full sincerity (which is always a lie) nor the Stanislavskian enticements of a '360° interpretation', nor a balsamic space of disinhibition, nor a pharma-pornographic sharing of intimacy. By suggesting the spectators to do something they can only do in the presence of others, participatory dramaturgy is not offering a collectivisation of disinhibition (which is an infallibly fascist feature) but the active and conscious form of constructing new models of shared inhibition. Participation is not bearing any aesthetics of convergence, but many aesthetics (one for each spectator) of divergence.

Roger Bernat, *Domini Públic* (2013)

Theatre does not need to pretend to sneak away from its origins. Like all mechanisms, theatre is a manipulating one. However, like all others, it exists to promote the hope of changing the result if we are skilled enough to be able to manipulate what manipulates us. And if we are able to accept that, once contact with the mechanism has been set up, any certainty that we are not subject to a manipulation just because we are its object decays. No public unmasks the manipulations of the mechanism without unmasking its own active role in such manipulation.

Pretending to provide an audience willingly enslaved in all domains of living (consumption, labour, and desire) with a surrogate space of unconditional freedom would be pitiful forgery. There is no reason for granting to theatre the role of simplifying reality by *dedramatising* it. Spectators feeling manipulated under certain mechanisms are just an indication that theatre is being actually participatory and honestly theatrical. (What is more, those spectators who pretend to share poetic responsibilities cannot believe that those things – poetic responsibility and the need to share it – are especially relaxing.) For if a freedom conceived as a kind of vacation is structurally false, a democracy the maximum deployment

94

of which is the lowest common denominator of the intellectual or imaginative effort will be a false democracy. Nobody has said that theatre has to *facilitate things*. Nobody has said either that, as there is no indulgency, theatre needs to be inquisitorial with the social guilt of the common spectator. An emancipated spectator is that refraining from the easy catharsis of feeling guilty a priori, so theatre takes on the mission of forgiving them; as well as that refraining from the good conscience of feeling a priori immaculate, so theatre provides them with the tonic of an unexpected 'j'accuse'. No matter how paradoxical it may seem, being a spectator should rather resemble a profession than a confession.

The feeling of freedom many spectators are assured to experience in the light of more comforting and regressive mechanisms is, exactly like in the society surrounding theatre, a clear symptom of the efficiency of manipulation based, more than ever before, on the constant distribution of a completely sensational and precisely *sensationalist* experience of freedom. The awareness of being manipulated is the indispensable prerequisite to constitute a hypothesis of emancipation. Theatre should not have a stale smell of incense, sacrifice, collective ecstasy, and acclamation. For if we believe that theatre is not the place for political oversimplification, it is neither the best venue for fabricating religious shortcuts to the socio-political complexity of present times.

The excitement referred to by Durkheim with regards to the expressions of community life is not a dismissible aspect of the sort of cultural consumption occurring in theatre and overall in community events of any type, yet it cannot be considered a purpose in itself. This confusion places theatre alongside those many 'timothic' (choleric) mechanisms that, amidst the turmoil of past history and the full calm of mass consumption, manage to use excitement as a means to reach specific (in no case collective) goals. It is by selling such excitement as a self-gratifying and hence self-sufficient experience that desubjectivation as the ultimate exquisiteness of the subject is used in a highly tempting manner. Given that such a marketing offer aims at nothing else than reconfiguring subjectivity as 'production of oneself through products', any use of theatre as a production means for subsequent *luxury subjectivities*, false consciences, and tinpot mysticisms becomes despicable.

Today's theatre should be the result of the effort to give up the abilities that have dominated the political relations between decision-makers (be they a director, dramaturg, king, president, or dictator) and the community. Adulation, understood as suggesting to the community that its worst instincts are also the best, will need to be given up as much as contempt, which consists of suggesting infallible recipes for rescue and improvement to the community. This would be the political precondition for a theatre that breaks down the paradoxical circumstance of a director perplex at being such who relates with an audience perplex at being audience. Only if theatre is able to conjure any bucolic nostalgia of anti-modern and specifically somatic community experiences (another feature of fascism), it will be able to create among anonymous spectators the societal occasion of reflecting on the meaning and the potential ambivalence of becoming a society.

It would be wrong to interpret the metalanguage of modern times as an abrupt irruption of the truth into the domain of fiction or of immediate action on the terrain of representation. On the contrary, metatheatre was a radical *epokhé*: the perplexity of a 'think machine' thinking of itself. Also, participation should not be interpreted as the circumstance under which the balm of spontaneity comes to cure theatre from its historical affectations. An audience acting not to think would not be doing anything different from what it is asked to do (and usually does) out there in the globalised world. Given that the dialectics of spontaneity and perplexity, action and thought is only prolific as long as it feeds on its infinite paradox, perhaps only those spectators are emancipated who, in the aftermath of the development of Western theatre, take over Hamlet's reasonable doubt; and take over the thoughtful honesty of intuiting that there is no original dimension to return to; that 'return', the implicit retroversion of the *meta* prefix, is always a 'return to a derived'. Return of adult theatre to its original lack of any origin. Return of the adult spectator to its original lack of any candour.

A true *meta-public*, the occasional community attending theatre does not represent the portion of reality called to measure the *terminal fictitiousness* of an already cadaveric form of theatre. The public is called to measure, if any, its own fictitiousness, not necessarily to disregard it. In this respect, the only community the spectators of a mechanism will try to constitute (without necessarily being successful in doing so) is what we call a 'project community'. Not the *radical* community that bases its cohesion on a *having* and a *being* that are shared beforehand (and often completely false), but the community 'united by circumstances' in contemplating an negotiable objective that *does not belong only* to the occasional community of spectators *nor is it depleted* in its rendering. The small provisional community of spectators will not achieve the collective emancipation projected by theatre but will only be able to convey it to the communities coming after.

Theatre should not add a belief or faith to the many beliefs the startling framework of reality is already made of. In any case, it should add doubts and foster scepticism, and there is no chance of reaching it as long as it pretends that spectators just accept to play because they *believe* in the mechanism. Two centuries of struggle have shown that emancipation is in itself the triple essence of the protocol of *permanent essay* that has characterised modern times according to Boris Groys. All in all, emancipation is by definition the script every generation has tried to embody, achieving it always and only partly; the *role* that events are nothing else than an interpretation tackled and relativized countless times by circumstances. Every generation has bequeathed to the following generation the history of its inefficiency and an intact project to accomplish. Emancipation projected by theatre is hence a drama the vitality of which manages to travel from one show to the next, from one community to the next, thanks to the relative inefficiency of the audience, which, like a circumstantial interpreter, has taken on the challenge of thinking and embodying it partially.

In the end, theatre is the collective fabrication of a working hypothesis that only occurs humanly when the awareness upon leaving the show of not having interpreted well the audience role mingles with the intuitive thought of the many ways of doing it much better. In a world where participation is a fact, yet almost never real, theatre should tackle the not at all easy task of deploying a participation that manages to become real without being necessarily a fact (or precisely because it almost never is it).

OPHELIA PATRICIO ARRABAL

PUBLIC MOMENT!

The time has come to suspend social boundaries and definitions. In a stratified, specialised, standardised, mapped, sieged, walled-off, heritaged, privatised world, which has been fragmented into infinite territories and ghettos that strive to acquire legitimacy under a multicultural, neo-liberal ideal, the public moment emerges as a collective ritual that opens up to all in general; it glorifies indomitable individuals, stripped of their submission and social, cultural, identity, ethnical, body, and gender shields. The senses of the public moment are activated by the sudden suspension of social inequalities and the confluent acceleration of multiple individuals who express a moving diversity.

In big cities, where cultural varieties weave into each other, social inequalities stand face to face. Most of the planet's population is concentrated, and so it is essential to collectively build and create moments that establish the city's public spaces as their field of action, spaces which are occupied by different collective bodies, diverse organisms that inhabit it in particular ways.

These bodies wander through a place regarded by the law as public, but which have basically been divided into lots; leased, sliced, and given out to large economic conglomerates that prevent common citizens from using that space as they please. That has clearly been the case, in the last few years, in the city of Rio de Janeiro. The curtailment of the use of public spaces is not a modern-day phenomenon, but goes back to other times and other forms of control. In the Stalinist Soviet Union all street furniture, like chairs and benches, were removed from the squares, which then became transit areas. For Stalin, the meeting of a community around a city bench was regarded as a danger for the maintenance of the compulsory ideas of a totalitarian State. The obliteration of social groups has always been a means to maintain authoritarian power and during the military dictatorship in Brazil this practice even extended from the public space to the private space, where any meeting with more than four people was regarded as a subversive act.

How does the individual, then, act in these controlled spaces? The subject always belongs to something or someone, and is defined in relation to the institution which allows it. Historically, the gregarious policies were designed for the transmutation of the individual into a subject: monarchists in the name of the King, a figure of divine right, representing the heavenly single prince on earth; the communists, due to the pacified, harmonious, unchallenged social body, in the monotheist style; the fascists, by respecting the homogeneous nation, the militarized, healthy homeland; capitalists, obsessed by the law of the market, the mechanical regulation of their capital flow and of the benefits generated. Always promoting the sacrifice of the diverse in the name of the particular universals they believe in: God, the King, Socialism, Communism, the State, the Nation, the Homeland, Money, Society, Race. In Brazil, there are uncountable expressions that show how the individual is despised, used as a synonym of unprincipled people, an element astray from the human world. That is why the word 'individual' can be used in the language of a police chronicle as a terrible synonym of complete anonymity. That also explains why in Brazil the word 'individualism' has become a synonym and everyday expression of selfishness, a feeling or social attitude which is deliberately looked down upon among us and yet adopted on a daily basis by all as the operating manner of an extremely competitive society. The essential difference that we need to emphasise here is to understand that, whereas selfishness is the policy of the individual/subject who only values himself, individualism is the policy that values individuals and their diversity.

And individuals are also collective because we are many to be one. The contamination of bodies in movement, the multiplicity of paths, ways, webs, plots, braids, tracks, and shortcuts through the interstices of the cities that harbour subjective diversities that tend to the infinite, constitute an intricate organic operational ecosystem of specifics that, in the hyper-capitalist logic of accelerated anthropocene, promote tectonic topographic accidents like social avalanches and eruptions where the abysses of segregation rise like ruins in construction, infested with steamrollers at work, crushing individualities, levelling subjectivities, and standardising specifics.

Opavivará, *OPAVIVARÁ! AO VIVO!* (2012)

Down here, this is how it goes: if you have money you go
by car, if you don't, you go by bus. According to the post-colonial
capitalist ideal, social upward mobility is directly related to not
needing to use public spaces, laws, equipment, and services. This
logic has been brought about by a long history of state and civil
policies that devalue, dehumanise, vacate, dismantle, and discard
as scrap all the public areas of community service. In Brazil, if you
have money you live, move around, and work in a property with
its own regulations and morals, armoured with mirrored glass and
air conditioning. The worse the individual/subject's social situation, the greater the need for him to submit to public spaces, laws,
equipment, and services. Having to leave home on foot to take a
bus or a train to go to work or to work outdoors as a street vendor
are conditions associated to the lack of capital, always opposed to
personal economic benefits like your own home, your own car, your
own business, family, dog, attributes that are valuable for the ideal
model citizen, and which are massively conveyed and trumpeted
by the official media channels. The most representative image of
this abyss between private property and public space are the metal

Opavivará!, *Cozinha coletiva em Vitória* (2016)

fences around plots, doors, and windows of houses and buildings in every neighbourhood in Brazilian cities, exposing the fear, terror, and violence that permanently structure this boundary.

When different experiences and ways of existence meet, acknowledge each other, interpenetrate, and vanish, we reach the maximum power of collectivity. That is what happens with the street carnivals that happen every year in different Brazilian cities, which, in a scattered and provisional way, promote remarkable experiences of public moments. It is then that the band, as a collection of individuals, stands out from the masses, as the individual/subjects' gregariousness. The moment the collectiveness is at its maximum power and radicalness is paradoxically the moment when the individual surfaces beyond his specifics, personality, and even his subjectivity. Erotic unfolding of all the internal materiality at skin level, like shoals of abyssal fish coming to the surface, decompressing each fold of their guts, unveiling to the air and ether the deepest caves of their skeletons.

It is at this point that we diverge from the classical understanding of community, which is that of the political parties that are today no more than teleological apparatuses created to take over the power. But what do they want to take over? And how can other collectivities set up different multiorgasmic organisations of representation that summon the other and are in a constant process of exchange, listening, transfusing, mutation, and contagion with other collectivities that inevitably permeate them?

In the context of the suspension of the social classifications, historic inequalities, and imposed hierarchies, the market and all economic logics are also eliminated, as this is the moment of abundance and of the band. The exchanges that happen between the individuals sharing this experience occur between values settled on individually and necessarily provisional, according to the desires, feelings, choices, and will of exchange of the individuals involved. There is no merchandise, only exchangeable objects. In this context of intense relational activity and emotional participation, the roots of what we can put forward as public art germinate and branch off in the fertile soil of widespread aesthetics that goes beyond the opposition of art and life, street and museum. This is not to turn, as is often the case, life and streets into new references and criteria but to mobilise art to a rising and expansive dynamics, envisioned to be always moving, wishing its amplitude and seeking its unfolding. Then, art as a commodity is just not possible. Instead, art will be a living condition. Mediation is difficult to overcome, but removing all barriers between artists and art users will tend to a condition where the artist is not a special type of individual but every individual will be a special type of artist.

And public moments do not vibrate exclusively in public spaces precisely because they do not have any exclusiveness or definitions of where, when or how they should happen. What makes living together more pleasurable for all is understanding how the spaces are built through the criss-cross of subjectivities and how we can intervene in them, distending boundaries and tearing membranes. There we can propose the categorical imperative of hedonism that considers enjoying yourself and allowing others to enjoy themselves – this inseparable second part being the genealogy of the hedonistic policy – as a type of alternative ethics to the post-industrial ascetic ideal. Sharing the world is a difficult task that mankind has been doing for several millennia. At some points powerfully unfolding into more life, at others destructively fuelling death. On a planet with over seven billion inhabitants, it is essential to understand how to get collectively organised to live in society. Collectiveness, the raw material for public moments, is set up by groups of individuals with an autonomous cultural, aesthetic, political, erotic, and poetic background. The power of collective manifestation is precisely in the blending of those people's varied knowledge and experiences who can together set up exchange spaces and forms of networked information flow which keep unfolding and multiplying action dynamics that promote shared empowering. Emotional telepathy!

The creation of such short-lived communities coming together through non-rationalised, uncatchable, random connections is essential for the setting up of the public moment. That is how theatre has worked from its origin, an ephemeral community that is created to spectate. But how can we be more than spectators? How can we tear down that barrier between stage and audience, wall and beholder? It is in that dissolution of space that the total can be found, a fusion of bodies in a scenario of horizontalities which allow for real-time free, public exchange in a democratic way.

At this point, we can understand how the public and private spaces attend and repel each other by understanding that, just as the public space can be privatized, so the private space can be made public. To create permeable membranes within those control spaces to accommodate and bring together individuals and actions that are usually warded off from there, is to build a public resistance space within a place where the logic of private power deprives us of freedom and narrows our vectors of choice and power down to negligible levels.

The permeable membrane creates a space of libertarian practices, Temporary Autonomous Zones that throb their full power and are parachute-seed shooting platforms that land far away and replicate the experience lived there in new forms and with other possibilities.

I seek the emergence and practice of an individualistic-collective, provisional and roving public art that can promote new meanings for spaces, whatever their private or public conditions, as public spaces, from the audience to the audience broadly aestheticised. It works as a force that de-compartmentalises territories. So, the most dramatic experiences, with a potential for transforming, inverting, and shifting points of view, are those that promote direct, multisensorial, multi-simultaneous, emotional, body, interactive, relational, and participatory contact with others. At this point it is important that we draw a distinction between public monument and public moment because; while the first addresses the masses with a closed, imposed speech, which only sends out a message and does not absorb or reflect, usually based on the common understanding of beauty and visual impact on the landscape, the second addresses individuals and strives to stand by multiple others who co-experience the moment, establishing a network of open contributions. The sense of a work of art that creates a single track between the author and the spectator is imploded and the sender and receiver roles are altogether eliminated. Public art should be open to any kind of interaction. It is totally permeable and that is why it is created during the process of public contact and contagion. It is connectable in all its dimensions; it is dismountable, reversible, and capable of being constantly changed; it does not start or end; it is always in the middle, among things, inter-being.

I am not me nor the other; I am someone in between. The rituals that stimulate the public moment, making use of public art as the trigger and means, temporarily suspend the secular disbeliefs of individuals and their tethers and anti-personification processes, articulating them in a collectivity that eliminates inequalities, absorbs differences, and glorifies diversity, operating as an ineffable ecosystem in explosive expansion!

ANA VUJANOVIĆ

THE EMANCIPATED SOCIETY

The new repertory is all about critical, left-oriented social and artis-tic propositions, *but...* Wait, it's quite unusual for a city theatre these days. Indeed. To be more specific, what they offer is a combi-nation of new readings – let's call them post-modern... sometimes even post-dramatic – of the national classics and more experimen-tal projects made by emerging authors, sometimes without any dramatic plot or drama play behind whatsoever. Plus, there're the shows more like choreography and performance. They're artistically divergent but they can all be outlined with a democratic socialist framework, when it comes to the socio-political positioning. I'd rather call it 'libertarian socialism'. That's definitely more precise. What I'd mention from my side is that in difference to the previous programme, this repertory does attract local audience, not only crit-ics and specialists. They're not always many, to be honest. But even if these people are not big fans of the new and experimental artistic stuff, they're nevertheless curious and surprisingly often willing to join artists on their journeys. Probably they also feel an urge to think about the current social moment in a critical manner. Because after all, what is the current moment? Don't we live in a situation that joins in a unique epochal knot the failure of all communisms with the misery of new individualism? We do, and here comes the question: What does this theatre do in that situation? What does it really do? Well, it thematises openly, more or less, the right-wing political atmosphere... it calls for raising social awareness... it some-times analyses burning social issues. But what does it do?, I must repeat. The audience watches these performances, perhaps agrees with the criticism and then leaves the theatre, satisfied with feeling good about taking part in that intellectual circle. And what then...?

...They were sitting at the communal table in the Landschaft café. They used to occupy that place, which was not a merely consumerist place; taking into account the clientele of the café, that table was also a sort of public place. A small one though, Magda would add. But still... The question of what Teatr Polski really does in and to Polish society remained open for some time. It looked like a knot that nobody was sure how to untie... It started occupying them. It became their common concern. I wouldn't say it unified them, far from that, but it did bring together several artists, philosophers, and activists who met in the theatre club, who have followed the new repertory and who have believed that theatre as an art form justifies its *raison d'*être by its social purpose. Otherwise, they were all different. Different age, education, social background... And now, *voilà!* – *the thing* is there and it creates a vibrant circle around itself.

1.

When the discussions became similar to these endless self-organised, bottom-up *perpetuum mobiles*, Magda came up with a concrete proposal. It goes like this: She thinks that Teatr Polski thematises social problems too much and really activates people too little. She finds that it mostly has an 'appellative approach', as she called it. The problem with that approach is that it usually addresses the audience who already share the same or similar social, political, or artistic premises with the artists. Even worse, it lets them go home after the curtains go down, with a good feeling in their guts, and continue their lives as usually. Joanna, Klara, and Mateusz complied with Magda's diagnosis. And everyone in the room liked her passion. Magda dropped out of her studies – a few of them by the way – and described herself as a 'woman of action'. Back in those days she continuously repeated the Marxist claim that art is not a mirror to reflect society but a hammer to shape it. Based on that premise she proposed to create a participatory performance, but not in the theatre building. She wanted to bring the audience and the theatre itself into the street; she wanted the voices of ordinary people to be heard in public; and, above all, she wanted to create a public stage on which they would appear. 'The spectator must be released from the passivity of the viewer!', was another claim of hers. Jan and Łukasz remained reserved – 'they were not convinced'. Others tried to understand Jan's reserve but he was a student of Philosophy, sometimes lost in the complex discourses he studied, and his reasoning sometimes sounded complicated. Łukasz was even worse, Klara – a gymnasium pupil and the youngest in the group – would say… 'He can be completely idiosyncratic in his linguistic analyses of every word mentioned in the talk, and in key moments it can be boring'. Since everyone at that table had already gone through the anxious period of running in circles, Magda, Joanna, Klara, and Mateusz decided to go for Magda's idea and write a concept note of a collective project that they would offer to Teatr Polski.

They could have gone for a completely independent project, but they still believed that public institutions, like the theatre, should be the infrastructures to work with and fight for.

The summer was long. Bydgoszcz could be depressive over summers… Almost everyone is gone. Łukasz went for his MA studies to Berlin. Joanna also went to Germany, to have an abortion…

It is September, when the whole group – except Łukasz – is sitting at the table in Landschaft. It has become a very popular place. A bunch of hipsters from the local gymnasium are playing cards at the next table. A designer at the oval table in the corner has a Skype meeting. It's noisy. The coffee grinder is adding its two cents into the soundscape. Despite the busy surroundings, the group is carefully discussing an offer that came from the director and dramaturgs of the theatre: since they were happy with the previous collaboration, they would like to continue with external projects and invite the theatre club members to make another collective project. Magda is thrilled. She wants to repeat the 'artivist' action they made in May. 'It works! It really made waves', she says. Klara, who plans to become a critic and curator, became more self-confident after the success of the previous action and speaks more. She says that she wants to be a little bit more self-reflective this time: *Abort your Church* provoked a heated debate in public but it lacked a more refined artistic elaboration.

'Why do we need a "more refined artistic elaboration"!?', Magda asks.

'Wait, maybe we really need it because we operate in an artistic context, in the context of theatre, no?' Joanna stops their dispute. Everyone listens attentively and nods. 'If so, than we need to think more about the politics of art and by means of art. Brecht, Piscator, Boal… they're all super political, but it's the twenty-first century now. Shall we still be happy with the "invisible theatre"? Hey, we must think about the politics of form and the politics of the conditions of work in theatre…'.

Mateusz agrees and furthers the problem: 'I think what we did was really good, and it was super clear and provocative, but maybe it was not enough. First of all, I think with that anti-antiabortion action in the church we didn't question the very institution of theatre, its structure, its accessibility, its representative character...'.

Magda: 'That was not our aim either...'.

Joanna's thoughts are meandering... She studied theatre long ago and worked with a collective in Gdańsk for six years before she had a kid, so this is not a new problem for her. Yet, how to address it this time, yet again, with these young people... who believe that institutions are open to us, that we are indispensable? 'I'm indispensable only for Maciej', she was thinking: 'For a few more years before he grows up and leaves home...'. Her future is becoming more closed. It comes with age. And although she didn't give up, she takes it with acceptance. Being reasonable came out of a place of flame. Without being sure where they are right now, she addresses Magda: 'Look, the people got provoked by the conflict between you and Mateusz, they took part, we made a media story, but we did it as an event, an event of everyday life, while it was a theatre *production*.'

Magda and Mateusz, who went far in the discussion in the meantime, catch her comment and speak loudly one over the other: 'Who cares about that?!' 'And who has the right to make that production? Who has the access...'.

Joanna: 'And under which conditions?...'.

Mateusz, nervous as he is, is screaming: 'It's all in the hands of the theatre! Its director, its logic of production... And nobody raises that question!'. He comes from an Orthodox Christian family and has grown up with a feeling of being marginalised and oppressed. Before they met Mateusz most of the club members had only a wage awareness of that issue... Yet Klara and Łukasz thought that he sometimes exaggerated and saw hidden power structures in everything.

'Ok, we can raise that question too', Magda agrees, 'but what about activating the audience then?'.

As Jan finally joins in, the discussion tones down and transforms into a sort of monodrama. Especially as he started growing a beard and now looks at least ten years older. But his point gets clearer: 'Maybe in the next project we should reflect ourselves more, and leave the audience aside, so to speak. That could be even more political. And we'd avoid patronising the audience for sure'. Magda doesn't really get his point, but since she wants everyone at the table to feel good and be involved, she remains silent. Klara adds that their self-reflection can also involve audience in the performance, whilst not being didactic. For that venture they must think about where the aesthetics are in their performance, the artistic work, the work in the medium. The audience is not stupid and they should make the translation from the politics of aesthetics to the politics in their society, family, and everyday life. Jan is nodding. Joanna adds that German theatre scholar Hans-Thies Lehmann wrote about these types of politics in art, which correspond better to the current moment. Klara makes a note in her notebook. Magda exhales loudly and agrees to go further with a new collective and participatory project, which – in contrast to *Abort your Church* – should deal more with the artworld. Finally, art as we know it is a bourgeois creation, and we should shake that bastion. We should shake it!, everyone confirms.

2.

While *Abort your Church* was a sort of *Blitzkrieg*, the new project took more than three weeks. The group was conducting research on how the theatre institution operates and how to create the aesthetic experience that involves the audience and challenges their usual ways of seeing things. So the project comprised a research phase as well. Firstly, they conducted interviews with the employees of the theatre, trying to figure out the structures of power, influence, and money flow in the house. Jan, Joanna, and Magda were very agile about that, while Klara was mostly documenting. But since they all had other jobs and duties it took them a month to make these interviews and one more to realise that the materials were not actually that interesting, since there was nothing really new to discover there. The employees always feel exploited and the management always finds them not working as agilely as expected – we know that formula. So in the next period they decided to focus the politics of aesthetics and restarted the whole project. The theatre was ok with that but started putting a pressure by asking for the title, an artistic statement for the web, a programme text, etc.

They were indecisive and proposal after proposal was discarded in their talks. But they all felt they were going deeper into the problem. For instance, they spent a lot of time attending to the question of: what are the parameters for evaluating a performance that strives toward a strong social purpose? How do we estimate its success? Do we say it's successful if it manages to involve people, if they start considering the performance as their own matter of concern and take responsibility for it, or if critics acknowledge its operation within theatre history? It's not an easy dilemma, and, if you think about it for a moment, it's far too easy to say: It shouldn't be 'either or'. For Joanna and Mateusz it depends on where you position your work: in social practice or in art history. For Klara, there is no alternative to the politics of aesthetics since art is after all a sensorial knowledge production. Otherwise, we should speak about politics in a narrow sense. The other day she brought the video of Francis Alÿs' *When Faith Moves Mountains* as a 'good example of participation'. Everyone liked that action. Its politics of involvement was clear. And in a documentary about the action one participant reported that in the course of the process they participants came to the important conclusion that we could do much more together than alone. Wow!

...Magda became slightly distant in these talks. Not that she was too lazy to think. Rather, she tended towards the straightforward action, while others were more attentive to questions. Yes, because questions, if we know how to pose them, bring us further, seriously, to the previously unknown territories!

One of these territories was 'social choreography'. ... And their new project finally landed there.

It was an open-ended event, predicated on various rules of moving and grouping 'spectActors' around the stage. As far as I remember, there was a big room – a 'black box' – organised in five or six 'stations', and we had headphones and followed oral instructions accompanied by the sounds of public spaces – the street food market, a tram, a classroom... I was split: the spectactors were invited to create collective situations that speak of unequal opportunities and lack of solidarity, while being so focused on the audio guide that it cut them off from the people around them. But it was consciously meant to provoke a tension, which might result in an open revolt and uprising. 'That would be fantastic', said Magda at the press conference, 'if the audience would destroy the performance and make their own!'. Jan later asked: 'How could they know they're allowed to break the rules?'. 'They should guess it', Klara reacted: 'It'd be really cheap to wink at them and say: "Please, resist, please, break the rules". Seriously.' ...Eventually, the performance was entitled *Choreography of (Dis)Obedience* and it left the possibility of disobedience open. It was a little clumsy but it was definitely an unusual theatrical event, which was relatively positively received by critics but left the audience somewhat confused. It's amusing to see how the critics were mostly waiting for other critics' opinions to say what they thought about the show, since nobody was really familiar with the social choreography. The audience didn't have that worry. For most of us it was an extravagant experience of contemporary art and many enjoyed it. In particular those who came with friends. They would chat, giggle, and remaining in their private circles they would only from time to time follow the instructions. I did my best but since the language of the instructions was not always clear we would often fail in following the guide and go back to our comfort zones of privacy...

'My problem is that it remained too obscure to the audience', said Krzysztof, the theatre director at a meeting with the theatre club members in the upper foyer: 'It was not easy to follow the plot line.'

'But there was no plot!', hastened Mateusz.

Jan remained seated in a big baroque armchair and started in his calm but assertive way: 'I find it politically dubious to patronise the audience that way. ... Who can say that it was obscure for these people? ... Nobody can really know what they brought home from that event, because there were as many interpretations and experiences as audience members.'

Krzysztof got a bit impatient: 'Ok guys, but with my experience I can tell you that the audience was confused. I don't contest the whole project. It's an interesting experiment and you introduced relevant questions, but it was confusing on the level of what to follow and how to participate', he said with the authority of an old-school-male-European-leftist-intellectual-in-his-late-fifties.

In the course of the conversation Jan became more susceptible to Krzysztof's comments. In a way, Krzysztof's critique fed his general doubt regarding participation....

3.

'If we want to continue working together, we should really be more self-critical toward how we set the participatory situation', said Jan the other day, when they were all, Lukazs included, sitting on the parapet wall around fountain.... After observing for a while the perfect white surface of snow covering the park in front of Philharmonia, he asked: 'Did you see that yesterday half of the people just got bored... and spent a half of the performance wondering through the space?'.

Klara sided with Jan and started developing a cynical approach toward *Choreography of (Dis)Obedience*. But she disagreed with Mateusz when he confessed feeling morally wrong for using people as performers: 'What we basically do is exploitation. We invite the audience, they pay for their tickets and then we use them as work force without paying them.'

113

'It's an ethical problem. But what worries me more is a political problem – again we make these people just feel good and do nothing', replied Klara.

'I don't think they feel good', said Magda, and threw a tennis ball far into the snow for her dog to bring it back: 'Our topic is too abstract and the people simply don't care about it.'

Joanna: 'It depends on how we shape the topic and open the space for the audience to get in.'

'Or maybe the very idea of opening space *for* someone is problematic', Jan said and looked at Łukasz, asking for confirmation.

Łukasz agreed: 'I find the whole idea of participation problematic if we speak about some emancipated leftist politics. To participate, to partake means to take a part, a part in something already set. It is like the problem with participatory democracy.'

Jan and Klara, who was taking notes intensively, were nodding, while Magda was profoundly puzzled: 'What is exactly the problem with participatory democracy? Apart from not existing?'.

'Look at the etymology. You see, everyone is invited to take his or her part of something. That is the bottom line. But: first of all, in what, and second of all, why only take part in something that has already been created and offered instead of building something together?'.

Jan continued his thought: '...something that doesn't exist...', and began slapping his bony knee with his hand.

Klara: 'It's a matter of time and temporality as well... How we open future perspectives.'

Łukasz: 'If I were to be here for the next project I'd like to make that switch, from the participation in something that has been created toward creating something together.'

Magda: 'I see. It's super urgent to emancipate people from that consumerist ideology of neoliberal capitalism, which is everywhere. People should start thinking more about our common future right away. Because we are building it already today!'.

Jan was gentle but clear: 'No, Magda, wait, we should not emancipate people. Nobody should. They are already emancipated.'

...This left everyone silent...

After a while Klara restarted the talk: 'So, we should emancipate ourselves to see that the audience is already emancipated; right?'.

Joanna: 'Pfff... I mean, how are we to interpret all these inequalities, xenophobia, hatred for refugees, anti-abortion law... and all other things?'.

114

...That was only one among many talks they had that winter. Over that time Jan formulated a thesis, which everyone accepted as the working hypothesis of the next project: We don't look for proof that the audience is emancipated; we take it as an axiom.

It was a deeply humanist and upright idea.

The third performance was entitled *The Emancipated Society*.

Everyone was in and somehow things came together in a very nice way.

Teatr Polski accepted that project to produce as well, which meant that sometimes they had to witness Krzysztof's thinking out loud: '...You know, if I compare how cruel and blatant the right-wing political agenda is, and how open they are with all that, I wonder what we do here with the performances like yours. And not only yours, we've also got the adaptation of Pasolini, Grotowski's crucifixion, and other stuff.' He would inhale his e-cigarette vapour and exhale one more deep doubt: 'But how do we communicate our counter-strikes with these works? How strong and loud is our impact on public sphere? I'm not sure...'.

The collective worked really well and, apart from having consultations with Marta and Joanna from the dramaturgical team, they involved two actors from Teatr Polski in the project. Paweł and Jarosław were in their late twenties, already with some experience in dance and performance, plus Paweł was a musician, percussionist. So it was a really nice crew at the end. They worked a lot, reaaally a lot, but nobody complained. In the breaks, which were sometimes long and mutated into another working session, they would be sitting in deckchairs on the sunny plateau in front of the theatre, drinking coffee or Club Mate and smoking for hours. Topics of conversation moved between the project, social concerns, and private lives, without real boundaries... Magda, if I look back, was maybe the most provocative figure there as she embodied her own libertarian leftist politics while others were closer – I must put it that way – to 'caviar leftists'. Magda was a woman in her mid-thirties, who had relationships and affairs with women, but since she identified herself more as a man than a woman she didn't consider herself lesbian. She would say instead that she was a FTM transgender heterosexual. I think. Moreover she didn't look like a man; she looked more like a sporty woman with short hair and beautiful blue eyes, something like Sinead O'Connor in the late 1980s. She felt that she was different from others, but she was used to that feeling and she liked these guys. She would go together with them to eat

115

veggie-burgers at Hamburger Platz. In the evenings they would go to Mózg (Brain), the only cool club in the city to listen to Paweł and his alternative hard-rock band. (Only Joanna had to miss the nightlife because of her son and her job at the radio station.)

It all created a vibrant working atmosphere too. However, Magda's passion was that time a little overshadowed with Jan's passion, which was of different kind. Burning deeper, like a wood fire.

The project they made was curious – they took a short novel by Slovenian writer and political activist Ivan Cankar *Servant Jernej and His Right.* What attracted their attention was that Cankar wrote the novel for the purpose of his electoral campaign, when he was a candidate of the Social Democratic Party in 1907. The campaign turned out to be unsuccessful, but the novel outlived it and brought Jernej's voice around the world. The other thing is the story itself, which speaks about an old servant, Jernej who spent his whole life working on a piece of land, which the new, young owner – who inherited it – wants to sell. If that happens Jernej will be kicked out without any rights and spend the rest of his life on the street. In the manner of the social novel, the book asks in Jernej's voice: Whose is the land? The one's who works it or the one's who owns it? That line moved everyone, and for the two months working on the project Jernej became their hero. And the whole performance was made around him.

After considering various options, such as a video essay on stage, a choir, etc., it was decided that the text of Jernej should be entirely delivered by Jarosław in a dry, anti-theatrical manner, followed by percussion. Since *mise-en-scène* itself re-establishes theatre representation in a way, all ideas were dropped and Jarek was eventually directed to sit on a chair in his training suit and address the audience frontally. Paweł, sitting at the drums would, apart from playing the instruments, recite the parts of the text describing the space, time, and context for Jernej's acting. In the monograph I read that only in Jernej's last monologue did others from the collective appeared on stage. They came one by one, symbolically and physically multiplying Jernej. They joined his monologue at the spot where they entered the stage so that the last lines – Whose is the land? The one's who works it or the one's who owns it? – were stormed from six throats, accompanied with percussions.

It was a very strong ending, all sources agree.

In the notes and other documentation, there is not much about audience. It seems that they were firstly supposed to act as court jury and the whole performance was to construct an imaginary trial. 'But then everyone will be involved in Jernej's story. It would be much better if they couldn't make it a happy ending, if we leave the spectators with the feeling of injustice, of not being able to make decisions', said Łukasz. From the minutes I'd confer that others agreed and finally decided not to involve audience because it would again enter the trap of 'taking part'. And on top of that, Jan added: 'It's such an important story that I want it to be clearly seen. I want to keep a distance in order to be critically observed as well, not to involve everyone in the performance and make them complicit in that way.' Only in that way we will be able to imagine a different future together with the audience, the group concluded, and someone highlighted this in fluorescent yellow pen. Um...

In an interview I made with Krzysztof about that forgotten artistic group years later, he said that the applause was pretty warm. Some people ended the performance with tears in their eyes. Others were a bit bored with the two-hour monologue, he was trying to pull the images from the dust of memory. But both reviews were positive. Not that they wrote about that show in superlatives but they acknowledged the work behind it, the relevance of the topic...
    'Nothing special, I must say, but it kind of went well.'
    After a long pause, he leaned his elbows on his knees and recalled the memory that still stays with me: 'You know, in the moment when the lights on stage went on and I saw those audience members sitting still in rows in the dark a bitter thought crossed my mind: 'Ha ha, look, *The Emancipated Society* just brought things back to the order! That's what they did after all! Pfff... and when everything suggested the other way, the flow of life continued just as before...'.

Any resemblance to real people is purely coincidental. The text – although inspired with a long stay in Bydgoszcz in spring 2016 – is a result of my imagination and the ongoing theoretical debate on participation in art.

TOBI MÜLLER IN CONVERSATION WITH HELGARD HAUG,
STEFAN KAEGI AND DANIEL WETZEL (RIMINI PROTOKOLL)

SPECTATOR REINCARNATED

TOBI MÜLLER (TM) *How do you cast your everyday experts, and how do you get them properly involved?*

DANIEL WETZEL (DW) One of the differences to professional ensembles is that our people don't always feel like acting. They have no interest in learning performance techniques. They take part because they feel that we have an interest in a specific matter and it's about working on it together. Sometimes we notice: hey, we do now give them stage directions! But in fact it's more about being on equal terms.

TM *So not all experts or actors want to become co-authors on equal terms? Do some of them wish more direction?*

STEFAN KAEGI (SK) In the 1970s, actors in fringe ensembles for sure also called themselves co-authors. But it's different if you take part in an improvisation with your creative potential or with your identity. Experts communicate very directly about what they have experienced. And some are sensitive, with good reason, as it's about their own lives. It's like a collective writing process during rehearsals, a negotiation, not like in a documentary, where the author edits without the protagonists. While preparing our project *Staat I* for December 2016 at Kammerspiele in Munich, a project on secret services and surveillance, it occurs that experts edit themselves completely out of the piece.

TM *What role does video play in rehearsals? Do you show it to the experts?*

HELGARD HAUG (HH) There are protagonists who refuse to even watch the documentary of finalised performances. They don't want to watch themselves with their eyes.

DW The fear of embarrassment about one's own image is widespread, especially with non-actors. Funnily enough, even with people who are used to performing in public – teachers for instance.

HH We rarely document during the rehearsals. If at all, we do it to discuss something again in the production team or to clarify technical processes. The basis for cooperation is mutual trust, having experts think: 'it'll be fine – it'll work out!'. Otherwise, you won't get far.

SK We had this trust in *Situation Rooms* (2013). It was very important, because for a long time each of the 20 protagonists only their own part, and the positions were totally opposed to each other regarding their contents. It was a piece in several spaces, with visitors stepping with earphones and tablet into the role of experts, who had partly filmed themselves and were now talking.

TM *In* Situation Rooms, *there is for instance the former child soldier Yaoundé from Congo. Do you provide room for a story, no matter if it is believed as it is or not?*

HH Of course.

DW Yes, but you need to trust yourself in front of the mirror in the morning. I know this as well [*laughs*].

TM *But the 'documentary theatre' category in which you still operate also suggests authenticity of the stories, doesn't it?*

SK The mirror is an excellent metaphor, particularly with Yaoundé. I think we really see his memories, though they are certainly, well, edited or shortened, probably very distant from what actually happened. The reenactment reconstructs what he wants or is able to remember. I think it is interesting to step through such a mirror.

DW   To a certain extent we all invent, according to the situation, and we all know it. This is why we don't talk of authenticity. In an interview on our first joint piece I was quoted in the headline speaking about 'moments of truth', and the colleagues were teasing me for weeks with the pathetic slip-up the *Frankfurter Allgemeine Zeitung* printed in bold.

TM   *In the end, you always tell stories of success...*

DW   ... you mean survival stories, don't you?

TM   *Yes, success stories and not failure stories. Overcoming traumas...*

DW   In most cases, we can only work with the people if they are in control of these stories.

TM   *Whereas municipal theatres are obsessed with failure, because of the tradition of tragedy.*

DW   Oh, I had forgotten that, German municipal theatres. We do notice if the one or the other wants to show off or not. But we don't do any parallel research, we don't send out any detectives or journalists.

HH   The protagonists look back on a tragic situation. Perhaps they reconstruct it, but they have escaped from it, that's true. Yet it's not finished; even if we don't invite anybody who is still mourning, there are fragile moments that are also extremely important and valuable for theatre. I can think for instance of the scene in *Situation Rooms*, where a doctor talks about his trauma in a way that makes you feel very close to him. He takes his experiences during the civil war in Sierra Leone to his flat in Berlin, he observes himself as he is unable to get rid of what he witnessed, as how they continue into his nights. By describing this, the audience gets involved in a very private moment – a shock – it's not over.

TM   *Failure marks the tragedy, and according to my thesis, it only works if you don't talk to people. Just like Jelinek. You always need to be able to reproduce the diagnosis of failure.*

DW   You mean that when asking people about different positions, tragedy gets lost as a form of description?

TM   *Yes. Perhaps it is because the protagonists in your pieces become more complex. Visitors reenact something instead of the protagonists in both* Situation Rooms *and the* World Climate Summit, *when you played the real 2014-15 Climate Summits in a theatre with the audience. Could we say that the visitor becomes an avatar?*

SK   Who would be controlling?

TM   *In* Situation Rooms *you are clearly driven through the earphones and the tablet.*

DW   You take the place of the actor telling something, well. Avatars are digital, I as a visitor am real. That's interesting: avatars of flesh and blood!

HH   The organisational and logistical corset in *Situation Rooms* is much stronger than usual. It's all about precision: the audience is guided or seduced into a sort of clockwork of actions, roles, and experiences and bit by bit becomes a part, a protagonist of it. The more simultaneously you repeat the actions with the film on the template you see on the tablet, the better. With *World Climate Summit* (2014) we try to set a sort of beat to suggest time and content-related urgency and how the spectators as delegation members can still reach the climate goals. And yet this is more relaxed than in *Situation Rooms*. Because you can also say: leave me alone, I'm off to the bar for a while. You don't cause any big damage, as there are several people in each delegation. If a single audience member decides to step out *Situation Rooms* it has a big impact on the show and can partly destroy it.

TM   *I have the impression that you are becoming increasingly masters of illusion. Immersive spaces, technical perfection, visitors as part of different simulations they can completely dip into...*

DW   Yes, but all this needs to be shown within its limitations. Everything is shaking. You don't move any three metres without feeling how everything is constructed in *Situation Rooms*.

Rimini Protokoll, *World Climate Summit* (2014)

TM   *It works incredibly seamlessly in the timeline though...*

DW/HH   It does.

TM   *There are empathic experiences for the visitors and actors in these immersive spaces and scripts. The tear in Friedrich Schiller is in your case the emotion about being part of another, often shockingly different world. Like in* Call Cutta in a Box, *where a video conference dialogue takes place with call centre employees...*

SK   Yes, Schiller is back there, not Brecht! [*laughs*].

DW   Brecht is! To be moved by something means to always have a framework that doesn't disappear. Schiller is framed by Brecht, so to speak, and in both cases they play – (I'm playing with the Schiller quote about humans being *only completely humans when they play*)...

HH   [*Sighs*]. Brecht – Schiller: we are now internally stuck in a big debate.

TM   *Performance studies scholar Shannon Jackson writes [in* Social Works: Performing Art, Supporting Publics, *(2011)] how she watched* Call Cutta in a Box *(2008) with her mother, that is, after her; how differently they experienced it, that her mother was indeed touched about talking to those Indians...*

HH   Yes, work inverts the perspective. It's about you. It's not about the employee in Calcutta, but what's going on with your life, with your society.

DW   *Call Cutta in a Box* takes place in two places simultaneousely, it's like mirroring. Both visitor and performer are sitting in front of computers in offices, at two different places in the world. Initially it's a sort of job interview. The visitor is thus in the focus of the interview, not the 'poor' call centre employee.

TM   *It depends a lot on who is sitting there. We know it from our own experience. As we grow older, we tend to stay in our own social bubble and feel touched when confronted with difference.*

DW   But with similarity as well... Here we're back to Brecht, Stefan is dealing with it right now...

TM   *Emotion with Schiller, reflection with Brecht...*

HH   Getting to emotion through reflecting.

SK   What strengthens identification and the empathic way is that we try to seduce people, not to throw them back by means of *distancing effects*. We don't have such a gesture of provocation. It's seduction, also from a purely spatial perspective [*HH laughs*]. That is, you identify yourself, for instance, with people whose values you don't necessarily share. In Hamburg, somebody left *Situation Rooms* and said: 'I'm not into it anymore, I don't want to be an arms dealer, not even for a play.'

DW   He complained to us in writing. We could say he didn't grasp the Brecht part, the *estrangement effect* – about which I insist it's vital also in *Situation Rooms* – did not apply. He wrote: 'you are manipulating me, you are controlling me remotely.' So this was an avatar that fought back, this was too compassionate

126

to him. His first station was a tank deal; he didn't want to get into it.

TM   *Participation is often seen automatically as something good. Yet this term has also been taken over by neoliberal processes such as activation, self-responsibility, and outsourcing. Things formerly done by the government are now done by oneself, but you've participated. Will arts also be into this precarious aspect of participation?*

SK   There are two totally different processes in our work, both of them under the concept of participation. Firstly, it's active participation when 100 citizens represent their city on stage or when experts participate in the writing process during the creation of *Situation Rooms*. It's what politics understands as participation: inclusion, taking part… Although politicians have no time or room to implement things calmly because they need to have the next citizens' consultation in mind. Secondly, it's participation of the avatar going through spaces and having a more complex reception than just looking and listening like in the auditorium. This has almost nothing to do with the first thing. He comprehends above all, he acts but gives no opinion; instead he chooses and sets the pace.

DW   Who now?

SK   The spectator in *Situation Rooms, Remote X* (2013) or *50 Aktenkilometer (2011)*.

TM   *So he's a spectator again!*

DW   A spectator who is always also participating in another way than observing from his seat. This is what our theatres were built for, to include citizens in the reflection on larger social processes. Schiller dealt with Napoleon and presented us with *Wallenstein*. Schiller asks: where are we heading to, what is the vision of Europe?

TM   *But Schiller's success is not only based on this role of dealing with public and political issues, but also related with accessing the soul…*

127

Rimini Protokoll, *Remote Houston* (2016)

DW Exactly. This is not radically different. Brecht just turns slightly away from emotion and points out the changeability of the situation, etc. This is why it's more about following thoughts and less about the noble and the ideal. However, in both cases, the relation with the public is clearly between the stage and the audience down there in the auditorium. It's only different in the *Learning Play (Lehrstück)*.

TM *In the learning play, player and spectator are identical...*

DW I have done some research meanwhile. Avatar means *the reincarnated*. I like this regarding *Situation Rooms*. It's about the fact that the Indian pilot, a general, cannot stand for weeks on stages and explain why he considers drone war the best and most humane type of warfare. But there is also the Pakistani lawyer of drone victims, who has no time either to continuously play theatre for us. Instead, they leave their episodes on the spot and you as a visitor incarnate this position, one after

Rimini Protokoll, *Call Cutta in a Box* (2008)

the other, experimentally, and within this framework some
sort of emotional experience with the situations is possible
again – be it irritated, pushed back, or emphatic. But then, the
door closes again after seven minutes and you, the situation,
and the role changes. So in the end all this happens within a
Brechtian framing.

TM   *'Incarnated' is a nice term for it: set into flesh, the lent flesh.
A very direct access to inner life, unless you are intubated, is the
ear. An entry to the soul, earphones have always played a big role in
many of your works: in* Remote X, 50 Aktenkilometer, *and now in*
Staat I *(2016), visitors go through a museum with a smartwatch and
earphones. This always presents something intimate and erotic to
the limit, as the voices are so low and come very close to us. This is
no public address.*

HH   Exactly, it aims at you, personally.

DW   Distance disappears.

HH   It's not one person talking to 500 people. No megaphone. You are addressed directly. This is precisely the subject in *Staat I*. While developing this piece, we ask ourselves how we can stress the use of 'you' in the text, how we can address everybody personally and manage to involve the visitors into the story...

DW   Or we can suddenly sing very gently directly into the ear, like in *Call Cutta*.

TM   *This closeness is sometimes uncomfortable to me...*

HH   There is a video recording in *Call Cutta in a Box* of a Swiss lady, sitting on the couch, holding the phone and bursting into tears. The protagonist on the other end of the phone in India is singing. This triggered something.

SK   We started using the microphone because our people had no speech training. Before our first big theatre works we did some radio jobs, for instance *Kreuzworträtsel Boxenstopp* (2001) with women around the age of 80. We appreciated the quality of the fragile voices, as if the biography had settled on the voice. The less trained a voice is, the more life is engraved in it.

DW   Audio tracks on earphones are a simple way of redefining the space without any need for rebuilding it. In Stefan's works with *Hygiene Heute* before our collaboration, at the end of the 1990s, you walk with a Walkman through Frankfurt, stand in front of a retirement home and a voice tells you this is a 'progerian station' where 15-year-old test persons are pumped up with memories until they look old. As a visitor you are a co-producer of the illusion, and in walking with your own glance you are also a fellow producer of a secret theatrical cityscape.

TM   *This has something panoptical, or rather panacoustic...*

DW   And also something incredibly comical. You know you're riding a trip thought by theatre makers, and everybody out there is on it without knowing it.

SK   It has a conspiratorial something. And it brings a secret into your little audio capsule. This is what made people so angry when the Walkman was introduced in the 1980s, followed later by the mobile phone, because they couldn't stand people wearing those earphones in public, typing something or even talking to somebody you couldn't even see: visible secret carriers. Western Europeans hardly stand a burka for a similar reason, as they are unable to see the face.

TM   *What is surprising nowadays is how little people, even spectators, oppose control or surveillance, isn't it?*

HH   People accept it – it seems to be part of the deal: you can locate, but you can in turn also be locatable. The lure is mobility and security – which is promised.

TM   *Would audio walks have been possible 20 or 30 years ago just like this, allowing earphones to hound you through the city?*

HH   In the case of *Remote X* they accept it as a playful instruction. Mostly. However, in *50 Aktenkilometer (50 kilometers of files)* we didn't control it and we did hound. The 'user' is not guided but has to make decisions – only on a second level did the user realise that he/she was being observed and surveilled from other users who could track and watch them. We used the technology there to illustrate and also criticise those operations.

TM   *Do your spectators look at each other, do they control each other to a certain extent?*

SK   All spectators are visible. In *Remote X*, it is choreographic instructions that makes the audience part of the stage design in the urban space. A staged circle, for instance, with everybody standing around a fountain. It reminds me of a parlour game. When everyone starts running, the audience splits. Many think: 'I'm not going to run with them, I'm not allowing others to tell me when I have to run.' And yet, 75% run; at least those who are good on their feet. The fact that manipulation is never complete, that some seek their own pace, is something the computer voice reflects continuously: it's the picture of a group that doesn't want to be a group.

HH   In *Situation Rooms*, all scenes take place simultaneously, but you walk through them consecutively. Visitors understand that everything they do will be done by somebody else after them or has been done by somebody else before them as well. Thus everything is viewed again from a different perspective.

DW   However, a basic criticism brought before us is: why do you think it's enough just to make the situation accessible? If you're making such a big effort to deal with it, why don't you sit down and use theatre as a place of thinking as action? That is, why am I as a spectator kept in such passiveness? Many things have happened in the last two decades, and most spectators allow themselves to be included in all possible experimental setups. Here comes up the question: can I as a spectator stand being just a recipient and not involved in the setup, thus preventing me from trying to take action?

TM   *Is this a generational problem or an ideological one?*

DW   It's a legitimation problem of politics as well as individual theatre critics: why do you believe that describing is enough? With us, there are different experiences; perhaps new approaches to both compassionate and critical subjects are opened. But is that enough?

TM   *This is the classic materialistic mindset when the situation also has to determine all arts. Shannon Jackson would now say this is in limbo with Rimini Protokoll: the materialistic and the artistic autonomous part...*

SK   ... and many cannot stand this limbo anymore right now. They demand to take a stand. Theatre shall now stir up and contribute to a more aggressive pitch, by which blaming comes before listening. But we do prefer complexity to polemic.

DW   Do you use the urban space as a stage or do you reshape it? As an artistic practice, this has been around for decades. There are new plans, also in subsidy policies, to implement artistic strategies into their political agenda. Urban Gardening for instance has already had some effect.

HH Yes, this was sustainability; this debate is almost over again.

DW Oh no, my debate is over again?!! A new generation of activism has just started to enter the theatres though.

HH To finish with a nod to Christoph Schlingensief: why should there be any politicians if all problems can be solved with arts? If arts could solve everything?

LOTTE VAN DEN BERG

THE UNSPOKEN CONVERSATION

Twenty 14-year-old kids are standing in two groups across from one another. One of the groups chants, 'close the borders, close the borders'. The other group speaks in cautious terms about peace. Deadlock.

We are working on *Building Conversation* at a vocational middle school in Purmerend, a small provincial town to the north of Amsterdam. Many of the original residents of Amsterdam moved to the surrounding towns like Purmerend after life in the city became too expensive for them. A plucky bunch of people in Purmerend. *Building Conversation* is a project I started the three years ago with the metalworker and artist Daan 't Sas. In the meantime, the project has grown into a varying collective of artists and kindred spirits, all of them fascinated by conversation. We see conversation as a joint creation, a collective improvisation, a work of art.

We had walked with the twenty 14-year-olds from the school to the local theatre. The teacher of the class, Pepijn, also came with us. He and Daan, who has accompanied me, are participating in the conversation and I am leading it. In an empty theatre space, a black box without bleachers, we and the class are performing the *waarden waterval*, the value waterfall exercise (it was developed by Humberto Schwab, a former philosophy teacher who grew so disappointed in secondary school education that he stopped teaching and now lives in Spain, where he has developed and is promoting the Socratic Design method). In this exercise you first converse in groups of two, then in groups of four, then eight, etc. The smaller groups keep doubling until you are standing in two groups across from each other and the entire company is participating in the same conversation. Whenever two groups merge, they have to agree on five values they share. We have come to the last step. The conversation is being conducted while we move around within the theatre space. If you agree with someone, you move closer to that person, if you disagree, you move away. So the conversation is a kind of spontaneous choreography.

The class quickly agrees on the first four values: family, communication, sustenance, and freedom. Both groups put 'close the borders' at fifth place, surrounded by question marks, exclamation points and words like barbed wire, peace and shutting gates. It's clear they haven't worked this one out yet. A tall skinny boy raises his arms above his head, striking the middle and index fingers of both hands against each other: #close the borders. Others follow his example while crying, 'barbed wire, barbed wire'. Some of the girls who have spoken out for peace form a group opposite them, saying, 'When there is peace, you don't need borders.' 'That's exactly what I mean,' replies the tall skinny boy. 'Closing the borders means peace.' The only Moroccan-Dutch boy in the class is the last to choose a side. Contrary to what everyone expects, he does not stand next to his good friend, a big Antillean girl who argues that there should be fewer foreigners in the city. He joins the group of cautious girls. They look at each other. This is getting serious. Everyone can feel it. Daan and Pepijn have also joined the girls. Deadlock. Nobody will budge.

A boy from the group that is defending borders tries to qualify their standpoint. 'Borders are also there for you to protect yourself. For instance, you can say: now you're going too far, now you're stepping over my border. That's important.' The group that stands for peace agrees, but this is not enough for them to want to move. Walking over to the other side is too dangerous. Then Pepijn breaks the impasse: 'I'm going to stand on a different spot.' He moves away from the group and takes a third position by himself. 'I think this is about security. Security is important – for me, for you, for everybody. I care about you. I also care about other children, other kids just like you. When I see images on the news of adults and children in the mud behind barbed wire, my stomach ties up in knots. I can't bear to look at them.' He describes in detail what he has seen. Children in mud up to their ankles. Scratches on their faces. A plastic bag to keep out the rain. As he speaks to the class, tears come to his eyes. He doesn't try to hide them and continues his story. Everyone has fallen silent. Slowly, one by one, they go and stand behind him. A small blonde boy is the last to walk over to him. Step by step, he walks toward the big group of classmates who are now standing together. 'Are you hesitating?' I ask. 'No. It's just that I walk a little slowly.' When everybody has come together in a single group, the tall skinny boy moves away. He stands opposite the group and slams his fingers in X marks above his head. 'I want to say one more thing. Fewer people. Simply that. Fewer people.' Then he stops. His long arms now hanging by his side, he looks at everybody. 'I'll come and stand with you again,' he says self-consciously, and joins the group. Security.

Theatre is a platform for conflict. As a theatre maker, but also as a person, I am used to digging into painful areas. I focus on exposing conflict, making it visible, so that I can observe conflict together with others. Settling disputes or solving problems is not my goal. The only goal is observation. Close observation. Conversation can also serve as a platform for conflict. A place where people can collectively examine, endure, experience the chafing, biting differences between themselves.

Several moments in this conversation with the youngsters are precious to me, such as the sight of a grown man openly crying in the midst of a group of teenagers, or the little boy walking agonisingly slowly toward the group. And of course the tall boy, facing his classmates alone, hands above his head, striking his fingers against each other to make X's. Bravura. And then his arms hanging down by his side in despair. Sights only seen by the participants themselves. Three adults, twenty kids; we all saw it differently, we all saw something else. But we all saw it, from the inside out.

With earlier work, like *Rumour* (2007) for instance, I introduced frameworks in urban public spaces in order to be able to look at those spaces and the people moving around within them in a different way. Now, with *Building Conversation* (since 2013), we are offering a framework – the time-space in which the conversation occurs – that not only gets people to interact but also makes their interactions visible. The forms of conversation are like empty spaces in which an unspoken conversation can be held. Actions and thoughts slide over one another. As participants, we have become our own spectators and the arts are our rehearsal space, the place where we can practice ourselves in relation to others.

TEA TUPAJIĆ

TOO REAL

TO BE
THEATRE

Part I: The Middle East

It is 2013, a hot July day, and I am entering the heavily air-conditioned Ben Gurion airport. I have come from Jerusalem. The purpose of my trip to Jerusalem was a presentation of the issue of the magazine *Frakcija* I had edited, elaborating the concept of the immunity of art. It is a concept I created out of dissatisfaction and boredom with the status and possibilities of art in Western societies. It seemed to me that anything that one does in art is always only art. The freedom of speech given to art has made it into a sphere into which all critical, subversive operations have been displaced and thus paralyzed. What I called 'the immunity of art' uses this weakness as an advantage and explores the grey zone between art and law/crime. I was asking: which subversive actions can be performed only because they are framed as an artwork?

I am standing in the queue, waiting for the security check. At some distance I see a young woman and a young man walking towards me. As they approach me they take me out of the queue and ask me to come with them. After the introductory questions – name, where I am going – they ask: 'What is the purpose of your trip?'. Unaware of the level of the security check, I answer, absent-mindedly, what I always answer when going through security checks on entry to the US. I say: 'I am an entertainer, an artist'. What follows is a two-hour-long interrogation executed by a total of five different-ranking and rotating officers.

We speak about my whereabouts in Israel, my family's religion, but mostly about the immunity of art, which they find simply by Googling my name.

About the latter I speak with a pleasant man in his fifties, who offers me a lemonade.

We discuss whether André Breton's surrealist gesture of taking a revolver and shooting blindly into the crowd could be appropriated by terrorists. They are alarmed when we speak about a subversive action disguised as an artwork. We agree that 9/11 cannot be considered an artwork, despite its visual spectacularity. We speak about Julian Assange's statement about China, where he says that the only hopeful societies are the ones that censor art and media, because they fear change, which means that a change is still possible. The West fears nothing, because nothing can change. The officer finds an article about the performance *The Curators' Piece (A trial against art)* (2012, together with Petra Zanki), in which we invited international curators to a fictional trial against art. We accused art of not saving the world, of losing every opportunity to affect reality on any level. The older officer, whom I have started seeing as my confidant, says that it's strange to expect such salvation from art, especially for an atheist.

Because they can't find anything and because I am about to miss my flight, they perform a body search and let me go.

On the flight to Munich I keep thinking about the airport experience. I clarify two things that thrill me about it. First is the palette of methods and performative skills they used in the interrogation. Second is that after a long time it felt like something real, like being an artist means something serious.

I imagine a performance that deals with the artistic methods applied in the work of an intelligence officer. It would be a durational performance/ installation with five Mossad or Shin Bet officers, each of them in a different room, each demonstrating a specific skill. All scenes would be formatted as immersive situations, they would include the audience as participants.

There is an important thing that stops me from even thinking about realising this project. I come from Sarajevo, the sexiest of all tragic cities. I always mistrusted foreign artists coming there, inspired to tell our story. It is a story that overshadows my childhood, the story that convulses the muscles of my grandmother in her panic attacks, the story that haunts the nightmares of my father. It felt almost like a theft. What right do I have to parachute myself to another

Tea Tupajić, *Yaffo, Summer and Fall 2015 with O* (2015)

continent and steal stories that belong to another context? When, after a few days, I do decide to go for it, I give myself two rules: you will not capitalise on the suffering of others and you will not make any neutral art (I wish I were in a Godard movie and that I could say his sentence, 'Art is like fire. It is born from what it burns.').

In September 2013 I move to Tel Aviv.

It takes two years to find five officers willing to participate in the work. I will not elaborate on the obvious difficulties of the process. It is a price you pay for the real thing. I am forever thankful to Leah Abir, Omer Krieger, Yael Cohen, Eyal Vexler, Yair Vardi, Paz Ben Nun, and to all those who choose not to be mentioned, for their courage and wholehearted support.

The condition of participation is the same for everyone. No documentation, neither of the process nor of the final performance. We work individually and the participants don't meet before the final event.

They choose the places where we would meet. I ask them to choose locations that most resemble the locations where they usually work.

Tea Tupajić, *Metsada, Spring 2014 – Summer 2015 with D.*, always early in the morning, (2015)

It is July 2015 and I am sitting with O. in Yaffo, near the sea. We speak about the airport incident. He describes the hunt for terrorists as a constant game of chess with the enemy. You have to think outside of the box, like them. You never know what the next terrorist would look like. Who could have expected that Japanese 'tourists' would take weapons out of their violin cases at the Ben Gurion airport in 1972?

O. says: 'With you it is the same. You look like a European, but you don't behave like one. You are young, but you are smart. You are not nervous, but you should be. It's like something about you just doesn't add up. I think you are a bit like an alien. You just don't fit anywhere.'

What is in it for them?
This is a question I have been asked so many times. Since I didn't have an answer I asked the participants. Their answer was clear. They saw it as an unconventional army parade. Usually only weapons and soldiers were exhibited, and this was a rare opportunity for the intelligence to show their skills. They say that if I were Jewish, the state would have employed me to do this every year.

And also, as D. adds: 'We have nothing to lose. Because it is only art, when we are in the performance, anyway everyone would think we are actors. No one would believe that we are real.'

Five days before the premiere in Tel Aviv I get interviewed by a *Haaretz* journalist. The interview lasts for nearly two hours and he seems to be fascinated by the project. On the day that the interview is supposed to be published, the journalist calls Yair Vardi, the curator of Tmuna Festival, saying they have decided not to publish it, because it cannot be true. These cannot be real agents, they are for sure just actors. He asks the curators how they can be sure that I am not lying to all of them. The article was never published.

The Alien
On the first meeting with each participating officer I felt the same mixture of confusion, curiosity, and suspicion, like in the interrogation experience at Ben Gurion Airport. Maybe O. was right; maybe I am like an alien. I believe that it would not be possible for an Israeli artist to execute this project. It had to be an outsider, an empty canvas without a clear position or interest, someone who didn't fit in any box, someone onto whom the participating agents could project whatever position they wanted.

The Tongue is Sharper Than a Knife
The First time I meet Z. we are in his office in Jerusalem. He is a man in his sixties, who greets me and uses a very unusual opener. He says: 'You know what I really like about you Yugoslavs? Your anthem is the only anthem in the world that mentions the traitor.'

I say: 'Damned be the traitor of his homeland.'

He laughs: 'Yes!'.

Throughout 2014 I travel many times to Jerusalem just for meetings with him. We never speak about the Shin Bet. All he does is recite poems in Arabic. He says that if he ever agrees to participate in the performance, his scene has to be called 'The tongue is sharper than a knife'. Overall, what he likes the most about my project is that I have decided to use the motto of the Mossad, 'By Way of Deception Thou Shalt Wage War', as a title. The emphasis is rightly on using deception, instead of weapons, as a more intelligent and humane way of warfare. For instance, the greatest progress intelligence methods have made were during the Cold War, the same war that had a significantly lower number of causalities then any

Tea Tupajić, *McDonalds, Summer and Fall 2014 with G.,* (2014)

other. Intelligence agencies are humanist. He speaks about the service in the 1970s, when the Shin Bet, to build a bond with the local population and to surveille them, had to learn the stories and histories of the Palestinian villages and towns, and the families that lived there. Slowly, throughout the decades, the huge corpus of the oral history and heritage of Palestine has been written down by the Shin Bet. He jokes that every Palestinian village should have a library of the Shin Bet.

I always wondered why people do trust them. They are all 'nice, well-mannered boys'. They all wear white, ironed shirts. They never smell of perfume, always only of fabric softener. It reminds me of what I've learned from G. about how to be an Arab: never wear perfume, but instead smell of sweat and fire.

You and I, We Are The Same
'We both create something that doesn't exist. We both make reality. Except that you, unlike me, can allow yourself to fail.' – says R. while we eat bananas in Shuk HaCarmel, on a busy Friday morning in the fall of 2014.

Tea Tupajić, *HaCarmel, May 2014 – July 2015 with R.*, mostly on Fridays, (2015)

I quickly write down the categories of relations between art and the 'spy business':

1.   Being an artist is a good a cover story: in a real event, the one Ben Affleck's *Argo* is based on, the CIA used the most far-fetched cover story for the agents to enter Iran. They pretended to be a film crew, shooting a sci-fi movie. There is nothing more benign and harmless than a filmmaker. Or an artist, for that matter.

2.   Creating/rehearsing scenes and identities as intelligence agents is a similar process to the one practiced by a writer/ actor. It sometimes takes years of rehearsals, in artificial environments that resemble film sets, to execute an operation. When R. describes to me how he plans his interrogations, I feel like I am discussing a plan for a stage play with one of my colleagues, including the *mise-en-scene* and the instructions for the actors. It is well-known that the famous Mossad agent Zvi Malkin has studied acting at the Lee Strasberg studio in New York.

3.   Cross-influence to and from the fiction – not only are intelligence operations among the most spectacular inspirations for films and literature, but it is also vice versa. For example, it is known that the CIA has a section dedicated to following spy movies and literature in the search for possible inspiration.

Tea Tupajić, *Ajami, Summer 2015 with O.*, (2015)

The Position

O. says that it is a shame to do a spy project without any action, so he shows me how to perform a 360-degrees car spin, in a parking lot in Yaffo. We stop in Ajami to buy meat at a local shop. He speaks Arabic to the salesman, and lies that we are from Nazareth just to get through a queue. As we sit in the car he says:

> You know what your problem is? First of all, you think that I am stupid. Second of all, you think that just because you are an artist, everything you do, even going to the butcher shop with me, is art. That's stupid. It would only be art if you watched me, and had other people watch me, while I, the evil spy, manipulated the poor Arab butcher. You cannot play some kind of double agent in art. People don't get it. Do you think the lefties at the performance will applaud how good I am in being bad? So, you get it. If you are not against us, it means you're with us. Get it, *habibti*?

In a split second this question opens all ethical doubts I have about myself. In order to convince the officers to participate, I restrained myself from declaring my political position to them. For months I

Tea Tupajić, *Azrieli, Spring 2014 – Summer 2015 with D.,* (2015)

have been pretending on so many levels that I am not sure anymore if the audience would ever be able to recognise the truth, if there is one after all. I swallow it all and answer 'All the time, Tipp,' as he pumps up the volume of A Tribe Called Quest. We drive off.

Did You Ever Learn Anything from a Spy Movie?
I tell D. that unless I record his voice no one will believe me that any of this ever happened. Since we cannot record any of our usual conversations, I propose that we simply chat about our favourite topic – spy movies. We meet at our 'location B', the sushi bar in the Azrieli shopping mall in Tel Aviv. He orders a soda and I try to figure out how to use iPhone Dictaphone. We speculate about what would happen in the next Bourne movie. I ask him if he has ever learned anything from a spy movie. He mentions a 'nice trick' he saw in a scene from *The Untouchables*, where a police officer, played by Kevin Costner, catches and kills a member of an alcohol-smuggling gang. He later catches another member and interrogates him, with the corpse in another room. In order to make the second gang member talk, the police officer decides to make a manipulation. He exits the room, takes the corpse of the first gang member, pretends

147

When it comes to movies, sometimes you can see some nice trick

Tea Tupajić, Still from *Did You Ever Learn Anything from a Spy Movie?* (2015), 2:53 min

to speak to the guy, and shoots him again, with the interrogated person watching the whole scene through the glass window.

D. adds that today, in a democratic society, one is not allowed to do such things, but that it is still a good example of a manipulation, of a creation of a belief. We laugh. After he leaves, I cry in the toilet of the Azrieli mall. I don't think I can handle this.

8 October 2015, the day of the premiere
O. says that he will be in the performance only if he is not seen. I steal the idea for his task from the BBC series *Spy*. As agreed, I let the audience wait in the courtyard of Gabirol – a centre for culture and art in Tel-Aviv – for 20 minutes. In the courtyard we put up a small bar, following O.'s request, to create a social situation, in which he can execute his task. O.'s task has two parts. First he is to use the bar situation and ask as many audience members as possible a question: 'Where did you park your car?', and record the information on his phone. He can get the information in any way he likes, as long as he doesn't repeat the same strategy twice.

The second part of his task is to stay present throughout the performance as a spectator, without being noticed, even though we play his recordings in one of the rooms inside the building, where the other parts of the performance take place.

Most of the audience gathers in the room with W. Her scene is called 'The Stranger' and it is simply W. having one-on-one conversations with audience members, with the task of creating a high level of intimacy between them. W. and I created the scene together. The setting consists of two comfortable chairs, for her and the spectator, separated by a small wooden table that has flowers, a water bottle, and glasses on it. Behind them there is a fake antique lamp, spreading soft yellow light. W. brought the lamp from her home. The audience is invited to sit on comfortable cushions on the floor.

As I roam the building I hear the audience referring to her as a psychologist. Indeed, after a few hours, the scene starts to resemble a New Age self-help session, with the audience discussing their most intimate issues with W. I can't judge if audience members understand the perversity of the manipulation W. and I have created, or if they are just so hungry for an intimate conversation that it doesn't even matter.

There is a scene on the first floor where the audience, instructed by two members of the Duvdevan unit, enacts a scene of an arrest of a terrorism suspect in his home at night. The participating audience is divided into two groups. One half is the military Duvdevan unit, and the other – a terrorist and his family. During the execution of the arrest, despite the soldier's special training in slow and quiet movement, it often happens that the children of the terrorism suspect wake up and start crying. The soldier is then instructed to take the child and say to him/her in Arabic: 'Don't be afraid. We are the Israeli army.' In the rehearsals we discuss how the 'performers' would teach the audience to cry like an Arab child. M. and N. say that it is strange how the same thing, when it is shown in a theatre, looks worse then it is in reality. They ask whether I think the audience enacting the scene might want to change it and, for example, have the child kill the soldier. I say that I don't know and I ask what they would do in that case. They say they would let it happen; after all 'it's only theatre'.

Part II: Europe
It is close to impossible to communicate about the project to the international colleagues if one is, out of security reasons, not allowed to e-mail details about it. In the late summer of 2014, at the risk of sounding incomprehensibly paranoid, I e-mail Sven

Birkeland briefly stating that I am working on a new project, that it involves the Israeli secret service and that I can not write more. We speak in the next days. Sven shares the idea with Stephane Boitel and Per Ananiassen and we agree to produce a performative installation called *The Disco*. Content-wise, it will focus on methods of interrogation used by the intelligence agencies. Formally, it will consist of the personal documentation of the time spent with the intelligence officers, an interactive conversation performance by one of the officers and, of the light and sound installation after which I entitled the whole work.

'One good thing about music, when it hits you, you feel no pain.'
Bob Marley, *Trenchtown Rock*

Every time when I am in Berlin I go to Berghain. My addiction to Berghain is not at all connected to the drugs everyone says you should use there. It is simply the addiction to the way music enters every pore of my body, making me move in the ways I never knew I could, taking me to the state between bodiless floating bliss and intense orgasm.

The core of my interest in the intelligence agencies lays in the similarity of the methods used by them and by the artists and arts. After the prohibition of physical torture, the western democracies started developing 'enhanced interrogation methods' as a part of the psychological operations development. The most notorious one became known by the small room in the detention camp Guantanamo, called 'the disco'. Torture by music is an 'enhanced interrogation method' in which the prisoner is subjected to music at excruciating volumes during a long period of time. The playlist includes hits of pop, hip-hop, and electronic music.

The bodily immersion into music, happening in the parties and clubs is perhaps the most radical form of participation we know in the western societies. Yet, we use the same music to succumb and torture the bodies and the minds of others. In collaboration with the sound artists Daniel Meir, I compose a 20-minute sound piece, in which we use the leaked playlist from 'the disco' in Guantanamo as well as the hits we remember dancing to at parties. We lead the bodies of the spectators from enjoyment in dancing to experiencing some of the methods used to turn the same music into the torture.

When we present the work in Europe, at the beginning the audience is dancing. Slowly they just stop and remain standing. The ones attracted to the dark side stay till the end. Most of the audience

Security guard protecting Tea Tupajić's
The Disco, (2013)

leaves before the piece is over, saying 'I can't describe what it is, but something in there is going very wrong.'

Billy, the housewife / Noa, the dog trainer / Lali, the curator / Shoshana, the marketing consultant
It's clear from the beginning that it will not be possible to travel to Europe for guest performances with all the participants of the Tel Aviv performance. It is simply too dangerous and in O.'s words 'too real to be theatre'.

I somehow manage to convince S. to perform with me and to travel to a few places in Europe. Before we even start discussing her performance, she drafts the security protocol that each of the inviting institutions needs to agree on.

Security protocol for The Disco
The performer in the work is a former Israeli secret service officer. The content/strategies with which the work operates is based on the security protocol of the Agency, therefore in order to present the work, we need security measures.

151

Security of the space:

There are two aims of the security:

1) *to protect the situation (audience and the performer) against physical violence*

2) *to make sure that people entering the space with the performer do not have any kind of video or audio recording possibilities (incl. mobile phones), with which they could record the performance and later expose it to the public.*

More concretely: usually there is a security person at the entrance of the building (or close to the entrance of the space where our performance will be) protecting against the violence. That security person frisks every audience member individually, making sure no one is carrying anything that could be used as a weapon. Step 2 is another person that takes the possible recording devices from the audience and secures them against theft.

In some European countries the security is prohibited to carry weapons. In that case, the theatre should inform the police about this event. The police should be able to react immediately in the case of an incident.

All security matters are adjusted to the architecture where the work is presented.

Discretion of the identity of the performer:

The identity of the performer should remain unknown to everyone except to the author (Tea Tupajić). In the concrete production/travel/accommodation process it means that all the arrangements are done personally by Tea Tupajić.

The accommodation location of the performer should be discussed and agreed on before booking.

Press

All written and oral press strategies should be discussed with Tea Tupajić before publication.

This security protocol enters the contract between the inviting institution and Tea Tupajić.

S. is a beautiful woman in her mid-thirties. She is a former intelligence officer of the Israeli homeland security agency Shin Bet. Her work in the agency consisted of interviewing the possible future agents and making sure they pass the security protocol needed for entering the agency. Or at least she says so.

Together we construct a scene relevant for Europe. It consists of her interviewing a person, based on the questions of the security protocol, while the rest of the audience is invited to observe in silence.

The goal of this scene is to address current changes in treating the matters of privacy and threat the West faces in the times of terrorist attacks. Namely, after 9/11 and Breivik the idea of the enemy changed. The enemy is no longer a foreign army that could invade a country with navy and tanks. Due to the growing fear that any of us, your neighbor, the person sitting next to you on the bus, the person selling groceries, could if exposed to unwanted ideological influences, and due to his/her psychological profile, if in the access to information or weapons, become the enemy of the state. Snowden's biggest contribution is not in leaking concrete documents, but in making us aware of the level of fear our governments have of us. Paranoia that anyone could potentially become the enemy is the cause of massive surveillance and data collection we are experiencing.

S.'s scene begins with her letting the person she speaks to choose one of her cover characters: Billy (the housewife), Noa (the dog trainer), Lali (the curator), Shoshana (the marketing consultant). She is so skilled and educated in presenting herself as each of those characters, that it is hard for me to judge if people believe her story or whether they just play along because they are in a theatre.

The conversation with each person lasts approximately 45 minutes. S. starts off with casual questions, such as place of birth, family background, only to move to deeply private questions. While observing the performance I wonder the same question as I did in Tel Aviv – Why do people trust them? The scene is happening in almost complete darkness, she is in disguise, obviously an excellent manipulator, controlling every laugh and nuance of her voice, but still people trust her. They open up about the history of mental diseases in their family, their cousins that posses weapons, about thoughts of cheating on their spouses. The level of intimacy is similar to the intimacy of childhood friends. After half an hour she manages to find out almost everything about them. And they still don't know anything about her.

Throughout the conversation scene, S. slowly builds a paranoid story, planting the seed of a doubt inside the person him/herself, that they could, maybe, under certain circumstances, under influence of alcohol or their own latent depression, triggered by a certain motive indeed do something they themselves never thought they could.

It takes me many performances to understand why S. is so good at what she does. Except for her talent, for which she was recruited already at the age of 17, professional training in intelligence methods, and years of experience, what makes S.'s mind so sharp is the permanent state of fear in which she was born, raised, and lives in. The reality of the constant danger produces the creativity of the paranoia, without which she and people living in her parts of the world would not survive.

On the evening of 13 November 2015, a series of coordinated terrorist attacks occurred in Paris, France and the city's northern suburb, Saint-Denis
One thing strikes me in reading the testimonies of the survivors of the attacks. When the attackers came to the café Le Carillon carrying guns, at the first seconds of the attack, people say it felt so surreal they thought this must be a movie. Similarly, at the Bataclan concert hall, visitors mistook the first explosions for pyrotechnics.

This is the difference between the West and the rest of the world. After decades of living in peace, the possibility of any danger seems so surreal that in the West one mistakes violent reality for a fiction, bombs for pyrotechnics. In the rest of the world, where danger is the everyday, no fiction could be less frightening then reality itself.

Before Paris, having security at the entrance of the performance seemed like an exotic adventure representing another place, somewhere far away in the world. (At our premiere in Bergen, part of the audience said they came to the performance just because they heard they will be frisked.)

After Paris, and later on Brussels, everything changed. Fear creeped into the body and into the subconscious of Europe and of the Europeans.

Now the whole of Europe looks like our performance, with security guards, army, and police on every corner.

TOM SELLAR IN CONVERSATION WITH ADELHEID ROOSEN

THE ONLY PLAYGROUND

WHERE WE CAN ALL LIVE

For more than a decade, Dutch theatre maker Adelheid Roosen has created projects via her foundation Adelheid|Female Economy, exploring boundaries of participation and a new ethos of intercultural exchange. Among her best-known works is *The Veiled Monologues* (2003-present), collected stories from Muslim women living in Europe, performed for a range of audiences and in different formats. Her more recent projects include *UrbanSafari* (2012-present), performed in cities from Utrecht to Mexico City and Juarez, for which participants are transported on the back of motorcycles from city centres to outlying neighbourhoods for facilitated exchanges with residents in their homes. For *De Oversteek* (*The Crossing*) (2014), Roosen invited a group of Amsterdam residents who had never previously visited a state theatre to sleep overnight in the prestigious Stadsschouwburg. The group arrived on the stage just as a performance of Büchner's play *Danton's Death*, directed by Johan Simons, was ending, introducing democratic realities into the fictional fabric and challenging official cultural institutions to extend their popular reach with new dynamics.

TOM SELLAR (TS) *Your projects often ask the audience to cross a line or a border.* UrbanSafari *takes members of the public to parts of their own city that they are often afraid of, to meet the people who live there.* De Oversteek *crossed a border between art and life, between theatre and social reality. Both projects, which are ongoing series, contain huge symbolic possibilities. Why do you think about participation this way? And why are artists in general thinking about this today? Because of a crisis in democracy? For a solution, or to form a proposal for a different society?*

ADELHEID ROOSEN (AR) My interest in participation started earlier. That's why I called my foundation Female Economy. In an economy, people earn money or they swap things. You can pay for a place to sleep, and you can eat. That's the logic. An economy is a system for doing that. But I never understood why, in such an economy, so little attention is paid to quality of life – not just what money a life can earn, but how quality of life can develop. What interests me is the idea that you are a human *being*; you are not a human *doing*. You do a lot of things – we do what we can, what we do is what we are. But that's never our focus.

When I was five years old, I brought adult homeless people home with me. Later on, when I became an adult, I understood that my mother was shocked every time I did this. First, of course, she said to me, 'Don't bring those people here.' Secondly, she told me that I had to bring them through the front door: as a child you normally entered your home through the back door. She must have thought, 'Well, if I have a child who brings those people home, then she should at least bring them in through the front door.' For me, when I did this, it was like playing with life. I thought they were my friends; they were on the street and I played on the street.

Who I am today comes not only from being Adelheid, the social character, but from practising an essential talent of being human, which is to meet people. I learn the most from meeting people I do not know. That is the best research for knowing who you are. That whole playing with life, was for me a kind of economy. A different economy, perhaps, than earning money, but that is the economy I was looking for and couldn't find anywhere else. When I went to art school, my performances were about these same ideas.

TS *When did you begin to think about theatre or performance, live performance, as a method for opening up new dimensions of participation? Normally, in traditional theatre, the actor pretends to be someone else, a stranger, and then we then recognise something of ourselves through the fiction. Your projects, however, use theatre and performance to help us meet and get to know real people, without a narrative frame. Your work is not documentary; it's an immersion in a reality, which becomes an interesting distinction. Your theatre helps us discover what's already there – what's already real.*

AR   When I started in theatre, as an actor, I found I couldn't recognise myself in plays. I started to write my own pieces. I came upon an idea for what I call the Adoption Method. Meeting a complete stranger is, for me, the best way to reflect on myself. I become shy. I become shameful about certain things. I hesitate, I stutter. That part of my being is for me the most interesting side.

I never use art to point out differences between people. I was sure that, no matter how educated a public is, they would understand what I meant in my essence with the work. In the Adoption Method, I ask my actors, as I do myself, to go live in a house, on a street, in a neighbourhood where they've never been, with a person they do not know, and to live there for two weeks. Then I ask them, what is happening to you? What kind of creative conflict are you experiencing? The 'actor' has to act as a human being – not hide behind a title of journalist or artist.

After I had led my *UrbanSafari* project two or three times, I said to journalists, 'I make a concept where you can fit in among people you do not know.' Because the framework is a theatre performance, you dare to go where you would not dare to go as an individual. Even if you hesitate to go to the performance, thinking, 'Oh, it's a dangerous neighbourhood, and there's a Moroccan scooter gang, and there's poverty, and there are disabled people!'. If it's framed as a theatre performance, you go and you realise, 'Oh, They are just like me – human beings!'. So the concept of participation was, for me, not formalised but a basic thing one does to live on this planet. For me, art is not a part of life, and yet art is actually the only playground where we all can live.

TS   *Can you give some examples of the kinds of experiences, exchanges, or discoveries that you saw the public having during* UrbanSafari*?*

AR   When I think of the *Safari* or *De Oversteek*, or *The Neighborhood Jury*, in which I made 12 people who had never entered a theatre before judge professional Dutch performances, I realise that in what we call normal society we do not see how often, within our systems, we are *not* participating. How often we do not *allow* everyone to participate. More and more people are becoming aware of this, today; economies, education, health care

Adelheid Roosen, *The Neighborhood Jury* in Amsterdam (2016)

systems are not really open to all people. We still have not found a system, a structure truly open for everybody.

De Oversteek was an idea of turning Stadsschouwburg into a 'community centre', a knock on the door of all the buildings to open up for people who want to see theatre, but have no chance. Is art for all of us? Or only for a few who can pay? What is the responsibility of theatre buildings and institutions? Earn money and that's it? Or find a way to collectively enjoy art?

I'm asking questions about the dominant, prevailing system. For *De Oversteek* I needed to create a hierarchy. I needed a huge theatre building and a huge director. The performance would not work without that. I entered this space with 100 people, halfway through a performance of *Danton's Death*. We entered into that high-class art of Johan Simons, into that high-class theatre building, with a whole public from the street when the piece was still playing. I made a procession for them, through the doors, through the foyer, climbing the stairs, opening the house doors, walking through the theatre, while the audience was watching the stage. They began to notice and to ask, 'Oh, what's happening behind me?'.

Adelheid Roosen, *De Oversteek* (2014)

After we came in to the auditorium, a lot of people in the audience were in tears. The public was saying, 'I felt like I was staring. I was looking and looking. I was staring, but I do not dare look at these people when I'm on the tram or in the metro or on my street. My eyes glance over to them, but for only a moment.' This audience became conscious of the fact that normally they do not dare to look at poor people, at disabled people, at a homosexual couple standing hand in hand. They respect their right to exist but they dare not look at them.

In the end we cut open Johan Simons' production. There were really famous actors on that stage. The 100 people I had brought with me were eating their soup as it concluded and at the very end of the play we walked to the back of the theatre. In a very beautiful, calm way, everyone found their place for the overnight stay. It looked like a marketplace. They were opening their bags, finding their pajamas, pulling out their clothes, re-dressing, putting on their pajamas. The people in the audience were asking, 'Am I really...may I look at that? May I?'.

But the people we brought in were just normal, behaving normally. I did not choreograph anything. It was just 100 people, putting pajamas on, drinking a beer, playing a little game.

Praying. Taking care of their dogs. Doing their normal little rituals they do before they go to sleep. Sometimes they kept to their own spaces. Sometimes they talked with their neighbour. Some took a walk across the stage, because they saw a friend who was over on the other side. Some read a lullaby to audience members before they went to sleep.

Creating that shy feeling, that feeling of being like a voyeur – that is for me the same drive that's behind the Adoption Methods. Go deep. Go real. Go there.

When I was asked to be on the jury for a high-class theatre festival, we were to pick the ten best shows from that theatre's season for a festival in September when all ten productions would be presented. They asked me to be the head of the jury. I agreed to do it, but only if there was also a jury of 12 people from the community.

We discovered that it was not the Neighbourhood Jury who were shy. It was the elite jurors who became shy, because they do not know how to be led by people who are less educated than them or people who don't share their tastes. When I invited the Neighbourhood Jury to participate, the traditional jury – who are all very kind people – began asking me for more information. 'Who are those people you've brought in? What shall we discuss with them?'. Meanwhile, the Neighbourhood Jury did not ask me anything. They were simply enthusiastic and only wanted to know the location for the meetings!

I discovered the same things with the public during the Safaris. They were so honest. They said afterwards, 'How could I ever have forgotten that these were only people?' 'Yes, Adelheid, to be honest, I saw the scooter gang coming for us with all these Moroccan guys, and I clutched my purse.' You know it's the whole judgmental instinct that tells you to be afraid of entering a household with a man with a beard and a djellaba.

TS *I see what the public discovers in the* Safari. *Can you talk about what the participating families gain from inviting the public into their home?*

AR Almost nothing related to art and theatre, but through making art and theatre they do get an extreme amount. In the beginning of our work, my participants almost cannot believe that they are 'worth' visiting. I could cry for that. But also, I can cry for the beauty of that, for the beauty of that space that they create by themselves. That space that is created through the cruel misunderstandings of being human beings that don't live *with* each other but only *next to* each other.

I could not believe in the beginning that the adopted setup would work, since we play so many days each year. But the families will not stop. They want to play more. They give and they give and they give. They open up. They do the job so well. We found a very simple form whereby they can repeat their life story in a very authentic way, so that the story stays true and fresh and open. They feel seen. They feel the respect for their life. They feel that they belong to life.

TS *How did you find the families for* UrbanSafari *and the participants for* De Oversteek*?*

AR Journalists asked me this many times in the beginning, but at first they didn't believe me when I told them: I take my bike. I go into the neighbourhood. I'm a little bit shy myself but I ring the doorbell. I smoke my last cigarette on the corner of the street and I try to calm down. Then I go ask whoever is there. (Journalists thought this story was a metaphor, and they asked me again, 'No, how do you really do it?'. But that is actually the process!).

I just thought back to what I told you in the beginning, to the game I played as a child. That is still what I actually do. I have no auditions. I don't do background checks. The ones who want to do it are in. That's how I do it.

TS *There is a possibility that the experiment could go badly. Did you have experiences where the public and the family did not connect, where the 'adoption' goes wrong or badly?*

AR Yeah, but that's also what I mean about values in life. It's a very good question, but for me, it's no different from any other kind of performance, with actors who drop out or are mis-cast. In the values of our economic system, we don't call that a failure.

For an example, Nazmiye Oral, a participating artist in the first *Safari* (in Amsterdam), worked with a married man who had a wife and child, and he was the head 'adoptor' for his family. During the whole adoption and rehearsal period, he was beating his wife. The wife went to the police. The judge issued a restraining order. For three months, he could not enter their

163

house, where the performance was to take place. We had to find a way to go on, because for me, there could be no question of breaking our relationship with him. Because our project is about this man's life. People do this. So you have to find a form for how we can accommodate this man.

During the *Safari*, we picked up the keys to the home where he lives, which he can no longer enter, from the grocery shop where his wife was living. She was participating, and agreed to give us the keys. We went to their home, and then Nazmiye told their story to the public. We would pick up their groceries, and then their keys, and then we took a walk to the house, where this man was shown on a television screen. So, we made that scene a little bit different. After the house visit, we met him on a couch outside of his son's schoolyard, because he was allowed to pick up his son. I never think, 'I'm quitting this story.'

In Mexico, we worked with a man named Martin, who was handicapped. He was the son of a drug dealer. He also deals himself, and that is how he ended up in a wheelchair. All this is about really following the living, right to the border of death and killing – dare I stop? People are open enough to talk even about the misunderstandings in their lives, even about why they were in jail or why they are in mourning. If they want to share their life story, I'll take that life story. For me, it's the same as in Shakespeare; Shakespeare also wrote about war. But when it's a real human being, then judgmental instinct flares up. People think, 'we cannot face this person because of what he did!'. Recently we made an installation in the Molenbeek neighbourhood in Brussels about the mothers of Jihadi sons. Faced with this human reality, everyone is horrified. But reading the newspaper, they have no problem.

TS   *These are the pre-conditions of a better society. It's not that the art event itself makes a difference – you're not building a new school or something like that – but the possibilities created by the exchange are what are necessary for a better world.*

AR   When we did the *Safari* in Mexico, which has a lot of corruption, we needed a scooter gang to bring the public to the home visits. There was a magic moment between myself and them. I was introduced to the gang and I learned about them a bit. I had to choreograph their movements, and I wanted a perfect

Adelheid Roosen, *Safari* in Juarez (2016)

line-up for when the scooters entered to pick up the public. I
went right away into the passion of creating and directing.

One guy, at a certain moment, came off the scooter, angry,
and approached me. I think Joshua was his name. He came up
to me and he said, 'I am the leader of this gang. Do you know
how to talk to me?'. I was scared, of course. But he had a sense of
humour. After a minute I said, 'Okay, Joshua. Let's make a deal.
You are the director of the drugs, and I'm not interfering in that
whatsoever. But *I* am, fucking hell, the director of the art. And
I need these clean lines. And you know lines because you snort
them. Lines have to be bright and straight, and that's the same as
what I want.' And it worked! We established a relationship that
lasted for the whole period. To create together in that reality is,
for me, the most creative act.

I take inspiration from Gandhi, from that expression, 'Be
the change you want to see in the world.' That is what you are
saying by being a participant. That's why I can lead so easily –
because I really believe that.

Adelheid Roosen, *Safari* in Bijlmer (2015)

It's so funny. In *De Oversteek*, in the group of the people who spent the night in the theatre, we had 16 refugees from Africa. It was a shock for the management of the theatre when these refugees said, 'Thank you so much! Since this project plays for three months, now we have a place to stay!'. The managers wanted to know what the rules were, what were the values behind it, whether it was allowed. I told them, 'Well, it's an artwork. And it's my artwork. And they are in the artwork. So, fuck you, system, now they have a place to stay!'. I love that. That is what I meant when I said earlier, art *is* the space we live in.

WOJTEK ZIEMILSKI

PARTICIPATION

AND SOME DISCONTENT

In 2002 I wrote a Master's dissertation in Philosophy about 'Identity and Alterity in the Experience of the Theatre Spectator'. In it, I took a close look at the concepts used to describe the experience of an audience member when seeing a theatre performance. My thesis was that (contrary to what some claim) performance as an aesthetic event does not fundamentally challenge the identity of the spectator. It was a fairly direct attack on ideas about the loss of subjectivity or suspension of identity that would supposedly happen during a performance. I used contemporary philosophical discourse on identity to question such descriptions.

My motivation was very personal: I had stopped going to the theatre, as I was fed up with a theatre that didn't pay attention to the spectator. As a spectator I felt ignored, disrespected, but most importantly – left out of the experience the theatre makers were having. At first it seemed absurd to question the very model that seems to sustain the vitality of most theatre (as felt by most theatre-goers). But I soon realised there was a flaw in most thinking about theatre, which is also connected to an age-old assumption concerning aesthetic experience – and that is, there is hardly any fundamental distinction made between the experience of those who make art and those who later see it. It seems enough to describe the artist as the first spectator to make it feel okay to simply tweak a few things and retain the same description for the audience's adventure.

The conclusion was simple: the audience cannot be taken for granted. There is no basic model of the theatrical – or more broadly, artistic or even aesthetic – experience that would *a priori* put the spectator on the side of the work. The work needs to keep working. One cannot assume that the structure of the theatrical event will create a space for an alternative subjectivity. The contract with the spectator needs constant renegotiation, as he never gives himself up for good.

Ever since then I've been working on the relation of the work with the spectator.

To open up. To include. To share. To get closer. To gain presence. To act together. To use the suspension of disbelief as a serious tool. To feel liveness. To blur art and life. To create an actual relation. To fuck it up. To have the actual possibility of fucking it up. To negotiate. To try out. To have others try out.

But also: To create a common space within the common space of theatre. This may seem a tautology – the space is common already! – while it's actually a paradox. There is no common space in theatre. No one common space. For a start, the audience and the performers have different agendas, different tools, different schedules on the day of the performance. They are two different worlds. The combination of the two can be many things – but assuming it's a community is naïve, if not blatantly arrogant. The term *heterotopia,* coined by Michel Foucault, besides being a space of otherness is also a space composed of different spaces. And the difference between those spaces is fundamental in the understanding of the space of theatre.

So, dear Wojtek, what do you want from your audience? To activate them? But you do know that Rancière is right when he says they're already active. And if so, what do you want from them that they are not already giving? Why have it participatory? Why look for this?

The very term *participation* implies that this (as opposed to others) type of performance experience is connected to taking part. To take part, in a ceremony for instance, you don't need to be particularly active. Sometimes you are asked to do something, but above all, it is your presence that becomes important.

Participation in theatre, the way I understand it and work with it, is an acknowledgement of the importance of the presence of the spectators.

There is probably not a director in the world who would claim he doesn't acknowledge spectators. And yet – the spectators mostly remain a hypothetical *other,* the very opposite of *actor,* as the one who acts with agency. So the acknowledgement may be the recognition of someone's existence, which is precisely the meaning of the work that is not enough – what we're looking for here, is 'to regard or describe (someone or something) as having or deserving a particular status'.

170

When scholars write about the problematic nature of the active/passive dichotomy, that is of course true but it doesn't necessarily address the issue of acknowledgement as recognition of a particular status.

Activating the spectators is just one way of acknowledging them. It's one way of giving the show the weight of their presence. (Paradoxically, it's also often an excuse to actually instrumentalize them and keep them unrecognised).

Why look for participation?

Hidden deep inside, beyond the pseudo-pragmatic goal of a world full of *vita activa*, I find – in myself, yes, this is a good moment to let go of pseudo-objective grammar – I find a need for community but which is a need for an extended me. Not being able to be other things, not being multiple enough, not through works of art, not through love, family, not through social bonds and empathy, I discover here is a chance to fantasise about being someone else. By bringing this someone else to a situation so close to mine that he seems to be my agent. The perfect agent who becomes a subject the very moment he comes into contact with the proposed scenario. And perfect in that he is not me, I cannot define him. And perfect in responding to the circumstances I propose/impose. The right people at the right time.

Naughty, naughty director.

Where is the freedom in such an agency? Where is the struggle for an open community? How can this egotistic redefining of the other bring about the *graal* of performativity?

Before I consider this, I want to think of something else.

Making the work an event means turning it into something important. Important in the sense of it going beyond the night out at the theatre. So something really happens. Of course, if I'm part of it, it really happens. Wouldn't it be enough to go to the fair, though? To take a ride on a roller coaster? Doesn't it 'really happen' there? Or am I looking for some sort of effort, of *work* on the side of the audience? 'When words do things'. In J. L. Austin's case words are *spoken* to do things. They are performed. Now is the time to recognise the importance of *who* performs. What I mean is, when the spectator says something, what sort of difference does this performativity contain?

Austin describes an actor's cry (on the stage) as 'almost doing things'. It seems to be doing things, but it really isn't quite. Maybe it would be better to describe this as – doing things by seeming to

171

be doing (other) things. So the non-performative character of acting performs something else. Hypothesis: let's consider it performs the possibility of a difference. The potential of the world. If that is the case, it helps to understand how the ambiguous position of the acting spectator can work on expanding the performative potential of the piece. The spectator is the agent of the outside. He is here to represent the real, the world, the thing-that-cannot-be-fake because it spectates (hello Descartes!). So employing him means bringing the game with the world – the language game of teasing reality – to a whole new level. The acknowledgement of the other, in this case, is the grafting of the tissue of subjecthood onto the organism of the piece. This inclusion of subjectivity has been written about extensively in relation to the actor, and even more so – to the performer. But the stage remains a stage and the spectacle does make us blasé as an audience, moving far out, into *onlooking*. Participation grabs our hand and pulls us back in. It pulls the world, *our* world, in a drastic way (*always* drastic) into the heterotopy of performance.

Of course, the world barks back. It's not necessarily a tame little teddy bear willing to be cuddled. It may feel violated. So many of us hate any sort of participation in the theatre. Maybe we feel we are taken hostage, we are being forced to participate in something we were not part of in the first place and to represent it, all the while representing the real, our real. 'I am not part of this'. 'I feel humiliated'. 'Do your job and let me do mine, which is watching'. This bear doesn't like to be cuddled. And even when it does – many of us love participating – it often feels like the bear has been drugged, sedated to make it all fit into a *good show*.

In a way, the above description goes for any negotiation between a work and its spectator. What changes is that we are now looking at it *from the perspective* of the spectator. So the participation is more a matter of focus than of developing some sort of interactive genre. Claire Bishop's criticism of Nicolas Bourriaud's *relational aesthetics* points this out by juxtaposing him with Eco's theory of *the open work*:

> [According to Eco] *every* work of art is potentially 'open', since it may produce an unlimited range of possible readings; it is simply the achievement of contemporary art, music and literature to have foregrounded this fact. Bourriaud misinterprets these arguments by applying them to a specific type

of work (those that require literal interaction) and thereby redirects the argument back to artistic intentionality rather than issues of reception. (Claire Bishop, 'Antagonism and Relational Aesthetics', 2004).

If we take Bishop's reading of Eco's theory seriously, and we refocus on the reception instead of the intention, this is actually a fantastic moment for the theatre. Not at all because it allows us to sit back and cherish the diverse reactions we may have to any given performance. Not because everything 'falls back into place' or rather, into the spectator's seat. No, it's because now as the director I have a fantastic new perspective – the audience perspective. The reception can be a starting point. I can work on it just as one would usually work on intention, concretisation of fiction, embodiment of ideas, expression, etc, etc.

And precisely because there is no simple, clear division between a seated, silent, and nearly motionless spectator and one running around the stage, I can explore the way the activity of the spectator functions, its dramaturgy. That's what I do, that's what I love, and that's what I believe creates a completely different way of functioning in the theatre as a place of experience.

That's all sweet, but how am I to work with the reception of a show I haven't made yet? And above all, *whose* reception?

The director usually assumes the role of a spectator. In the world of participatory performance, that can hardly be the case.

I usually invite people to experience the show. It's what would normally be a work-in-progress, only here it feels more like a strange laboratory. The intimate and the manipulative, the directed and the open come together. In a recent production we would call the invited guests 'rabbits', like lab rabbits (a Polish, nicer term for lab rats), because they were put in this maze and observed. How else are we to know what the reception is? How can we work on it flexibly?

At times it feels like a focus group in a company producing soap. The element of 'market research'. Possibly the feeling has more to do with our associations than with the actual contexts. After all, testing happens also in non-commercial circumstances.

But the tension between what should be and is to be predicted and what should be left open remains. It is often the most important part – the delicately oscillating pendulum of agency.

For a while I had an obsession with agency. Give them power! Free them, don't turn them into functionaries! Then one day I was playing a game and I realised I could be called a functionary of the game. The reason I'm not is because I know the rules and I don't feel imprisoned in them. (If it's a good game. If not, that is exactly how I may feel). The agency I could find even in a simple board game is not just about the game itself and my role in it. It's also (maybe mainly) about how the game functions within the ecosystem I'm in. It allows me to be with other people, to rework our language games, to combine my social role with a superficial, short-term, mainly fictional function I have in the game. Last but not least, the agency of the game develops through the dramaturgy of the event it creates.

I wish I had a smart conclusion that would put it all in place. I'm afraid I'm in the middle of rehearsals now, and combining these two processes of thought is killing my brain, it's like making a show and at the same time daydreaming about spectators moving in and taking part.

So let me finish with a list of complaints about a lot of participatory work.

Problem #1 with participation:
Things get too intimate.

You go to see a show. At some point of the show, the actors start encouraging people to talk to them directly, somewhere offstage. It happens. Then the show resumes. And you feel something is wrong. The 'truth' of the meeting seems fake now, like it was forced into the structure, which chewed through it and spat it out like tobacco.

Even if the show doesn't resume, you clap at the end. Or you read a review in the press. What was meant to be hidden away in the safety of a participatory act is still part of the world. No, seriously: not every date needs to stay offline, but can't we allow it once in a while?

Problem #2 with participation:
Things don't get intimate.

We ain't got a thing goin' on. No sparks. Participation without the sparks is like any other affective model without the affect – dull. So the smartest participatory performance can be a total disaster, maybe more so than the smartest non-participatory performance. Because it is so dependent on the affect, on the letting go and opening up to the experience.

Problem #3 with participation:
The spectators only matter as props. [Fake agency].

You're encouraged to stand where you want during the show. You're asked to move to a different space every once in a while. Problem is, it doesn't change a thing. Certainly not to you. Possibly, it changes something to the other members of the audience, for whom you become a prop in the show, or an extra. But that's not empowerment or acknowledgement, that's using you. While conveniently assuming you want to go through that tunnel and hold that candle and talk to your neighbour. This is different from Problem #2 because it's not about affect, it's about accepting agency.

Problem #4 with participation:
The loss of symbolism.

Yes, the conversation with the actor was great. And the dancing together was very pleasant. And yet, for some reason it feels poor. Like you've lost something along the way. The art stopped having the additional power – an aura, or a form of symbolism – the power to be much more than what it seemingly is. The work became so close to you, so down-to-earth, that it's hard to feel it as moving (you) somewhere else.

This goes to some extent along the lines of Rancière's critique of the ideas of 'activating' the spectator – they tend to make it impossible to really take part, as you are too much inside to be able to see much. So there is no possibility of overview (or maybe, no V-effekt?).

My issue with this description is that it also assumes there is no possibility of being both inside and outside at the same time. We do it when sitting on the seat, why assume it to be fundamentally impossible somewhere else? But something indeed may be lost – it is the notion of representation as mimesis, but not as a mirror image, only a reflection of another reality. Going from the outside onto the stage is a radical shift. When the movement is accompanied by a destruction of the difference, the radicality vanishes.

Problem #5 with participation:

Words words words.

Just shut up already. Do your thing. You don't need to make me part of everything, really. When Deleuze said art has nothing to do with communication ('at all!'), well, it should make us think.

Problem #6:

Exclusivity.

It drives me mad when the work claims to be universalist while sticking to the safest audience possible and using them as representants of Spectatorship.

It works because I know half of the audience. It's universal because the target universe is tiny. It's open to any interpretation because we've read the same books that show us the scope. This is extremely common with a lot of engaged art, but it's particularly disturbing in participatory work.

Problem #7:

Inclusiveness

Who should participate? The audience? All of them? Some of them? One of them? The whole challenge is to build a dramaturgy of participation. How are we not to assume things about the audience? And why shouldn't we?

Problem #8:

Everything is political.

Yes, we know. And yet it isn't. Not until you make it so. And if you really insist – really, really, turning every participatory procedure into a way of proving your wise political stance – you may just end up like the guy at the party who spends all night complaining about politics, until you regret you've even shown up at the party. Is he right? By then no one cares. Can we make an analogy between a party and a performance? I just did. But isn't performance significantly different from a party? Yes, that's why it's called an analogy.

Problem #9:

Participate or else.

There is always more participation available just around the corner. The whole theatrical device seems to encourage overcoming the static contemplative position and somehow getting more involved.

I would call it the spinning top paradox. My one-year-old son loves the spinning top. Every single day he asks me to spin the colorful toy. For a few seconds after I let go, he looks on, seemingly mesmerised. But this lasts only a short instant – he quickly proceeds to try and interact with the toy, making it stop spinning.

Performance is often like the spinning top – it seems to point towards participation. It looks like the structure only needs another step to engage so much more, to produce so much more, to allow so very much more. Yet when that happens, it – well, I wouldn't dramatise and claim that it's all gone, then. It just seldom delivers the experience that it announces or proposes.

I have been witness to an example of this. It was a performance by an artist I have the highest regard for – Paweł Althamer. And it failed. The idea was to bring the (unaware) audience of the performance to a TV studio, and have them create an actual TV programme (shown afterwards on a cultural TV station). The spectators – meticulously isolated from any hint of what was to come – suddenly found themselves in a professional TV studio, with costumes at their disposal, make-up people, cameramen. And it was up to the spectators/participants to define what would happen. What actually did happen was a struggle to survive through a desperate reproduction of talk-show formats. The spinning top stopped abruptly.

At a certain point of the performance the artist himself joined the spectators and a discussion followed about the aim of the project. 'I wanted to see what would happen if we switched the roles', I remember him saying.

The problem was – nobody there had the tools to build something out of this. The *ad hoc* proposal turned everyone into complete dilettantes, and the magic did not happen. The need for communion, for overcoming the distance of the spectator – for participation was just not enough for it to work.

Problem #10:
Losing grip of reality (overperformativity, or: believing yourself when you say you want people to step out of the theatre and change the world).

Prolog is a performance I directed in 2012. It is about spectatorship. It's performed for 12 (sometimes up to 15) spectators who are alone on the stage, wearing earphones where they hear instructions to a simple game they are playing. The final scene is a fantasy

177

about the audience. The potential to go beyond theatre is always present. After all, this is a group of people gathered in a specific space who share an aesthetic experience. They are summoned for an event whose liveness and immediacy supposedly defines them, or at least brings them together, as a collective. Couldn't they take matters in their own hands?

In one show, at the PACT Zollverein in Essen, they did. Several spectators stayed at the end of the show and refused to leave the stage. This happened during the time of the Occupy movement and was a clear 'Occupy Theatre' initiative. Was this the realisation of the fantasy? Was that the point? Was that the ultimate performative gesture – the *'passage a l'acte'*?

For me as the director it became clear, during this situation, that it was a miss. Maybe because I was not calling to arms. I was simply pointing to this potential. What would they gather around? What could they change? The Occupy Theatre ended rather quickly. What was crucial, though, was a talk we had after each show, to be able to establish the possible performative power of such a situation.

Staying on the stage is easy. Working out a possible outcome is the challenge.

In other words – participation is easy. The creation of a new energy is the challenge.

ADAM CZIRAK IN CONVERSATION WITH JOHANNA FREIBURG
AND BASTIAN TROST (GOB SQUAD)

IT COULD HAVE BEEN ME!

Participation plays an important role at many different levels in the productions of the Gob Squad Performance Collective. The way of developing a piece is already the result of a shared decision-making process of the seven group members. One of the most famous distinctive features of Gob Squad lies, however, in the fact that their performances seldom do without the involvement of the spectators or passers-by in the public space. The performers Johanna Freiburg and Bastian Trost speak about the aesthetics and politics of participation in Gob Squad.

ADAM CZIRAK (AC) *You improvise and develop the plays in a way that you frequently change your roles and mutually profit from the developed ideas. A scenic idea unfolded by one of you can later be picked up and appropriated by someone else. How does participating in each other's ideas work and can we still speak of dimensions of the individual, the self, the irreplaceable in the context of this collective work practice?*

JOHANNA FREIBURG (JF) Our productions always have more performers involved than it would be necessary based on the available roles, so that we can change between the inside and the outside position. Thus we can change the perspective between the experience of contributing to a scene and the position arising from the critical distance of 'looking from above'. These changes are at the heart of our rehearsal process. As a result, the roles and the tasks are growing with time so that each of us brings in our very personal way to perform, giving way to a collective authorship. This collective authorship actually means that it is permitted to pick up things from the others, as well as

181

to repeat, to copy, and to change them. Accordingly, our work consists of a mixture of moments that are predefined and fixed dramaturgically and therefore only vary slightly in the individual shows on the one hand, and of moments that can differ more and be performed freely by the performers on the other hand. Can we put it that way?

BASTIAN TROST (BT) Yes. I am thinking about what cannot be replaced. When I was new in Gob Squad, I as an actor was wondering about the craft and the specific skills of a performer. Within the group it became clear that none of us aspired to have a specific craft that only s/he could master and the others couldn't. With the passing of time I have the feeling that the craft in Gob Squad consists of being a playwright, a performer, an author and a spectator at the same time. Whereas everyone standing on stage of a theatre elsewhere tend to have a specific talent or must have a particular craft. When performing arts are developing in the direction of circus, it is even more about having an ability where the spectator says: 'Wow, I could never do that!'. But we would rather have them saying 'Oh, this is so easy, I could also do that!'. Often the performer makes himself even more vulnerable than the spectator so that no hierarchical sense of expertise can arise. Therefore, we pay attention to the fact that there would be no scenes, in which a specific performer, who can sing or play an instrument particularly well, shows his or her ability. It is not desirable that a certain role could only be played by a specific performer. The interchangeability is very important to us. And the only thing that is not replaceable are the personal stories which we fill a role with, but the fact *that* a personal story comes up, is again interchangeable. In fact, everything is interchangeable except for the structure of the play that we have developed together.

JF   Everything is indeed interchangeable, because everyone is replaceable. We have never developed a piece in which someone would be indispensable. But it does not mean that there are no agreements beforehand. This would mean that a role or a character would be open to free interpretation. Interestingly, a character is being shaped only in the continuous process of our sharing and constant changing of roles. It is often misunderstood why we are working with varying casts, because it is seldom considered to be the core of our working concept.

Even programmers, who see a play from us for the first time, assume that they have seen the best cast. When they invite us to a guest performance and we play there in any other constellation, they automatically think that they are getting a cast B or C. In our way of thinking that is absolutely not the case.

AC *How does the cast for a specific production come together? You work regularly with guest performers. What factors are involved in their selection for a particular production?*

JF In Gob Squad basically everybody is involved in the process. And this is always more than we need in an economic sense, more than the characters or roles on stage.

BT With the guest performers there is a project-specific consideration and a careful selection. But it also has a lot to do with sympathy and with the question of how someone is able to ᾿t in the collective work.

AC *Mᴜ⸻ of your pieces are designed in a way that members of the audience can replace you or can be cast for certain roles. With this principle of replacement you also delegate a certain responsibility. How can you prepare yourselves for these participatory scenes?*

JF Reflecting on the role of the spectators is the most important thing for us. In the case of each new concept we ask ourselves again and again how the relationship with the audience should be organised. When we have ideas for the participation, we try them beforehand amongst us by playing the spectators to see if the idea has potential. We often have assistants, guests, or people involved in the production like costume designers, who we ask to enter the situation. It is always very important to invite test audiences right from our early rehearsals, and these 'try outs' work best, when we don't know the spectators and we all come to the situation as a fresh encounter. In case of some productions, there are around 10-30 spectators sitting in our run-throughs towards the end of the rehearsal period helping us to get a feeling for the participative scenes. Even on the first night we do not reach a final point of the artistic process, because our relationship with the audience is something that we learn about only during performances.

Gob Squad, *Gob Squad's Kitchen* (2007)

BT   What I find important to mention is that the conception of a performance always provides a part for the spectators, no matter whether they are actually active or not. As a member of the audience you play a part, for instance, in *Revolution Now!*, as we assume that you are here tonight, among other things, because of the title. You came here because you want a revolution. So even if you are not filmed, if you are not involved in the dialogue, you do have a role you are playing, one we have already given to you. It means that also the passive role of the spectator is at stake. And that helps us to have a justification for the evening. The audience has – as much as we have – a function. They play a role and their fantasies are involved. And it is absolutely not essential that this spectator fantasy leads to an actual participation. In *Gob Squad's Kitchen* only four spectators come de facto out on stage, but in our conception they are all playing a part.

Gob Squad, *Western Society* (2013)

JF   Yes, because there is something like a proxy principle for the spectator. You think, 'that could have been me'. And that's a very important aspect of participation, since you, as a spectator yourself, have a completely different view of the participants, you empathise with them. The dividing line between performing and watching becomes thus more blurred.

BT   Our performances contain tasks and everyone wonders how they could possibly have fulfilled this task. However, the spectators are sometimes suspicious and assume that everything is fully rehearsed and the participation is in fact a fake one. You could feel that in *Kitchen*, because many would not believe that the co-players from the audience were real spectators. *Western Society* is a reaction to that – an attempt to make the selection more transparent, to show that here someone is really chosen arbitrarily. Since our concept only functions when people see that those co-players are real spectators.

AC   *You often interact with passers-by in a public place by addressing them and trying to win them into the ongoing show as performers, while the audience in the theatre are watching the casting through live video. This strategy could be described as an enticement to participation. What always captivates me as a spectator are the moments when neither you, nor the audience can be sure that the addressed passer-by is willing to get involved into the play.*

BT   It's as if you are watching somebody doing a lot of persuading, when one tries to coax a passer-by into doing something. When you watch a play several times, you will notice that different performers have different strategies.

JF   These efforts of persuasion are about someone exceeding their own frontiers, diverging from their own way, or doing something unexpected or extraordinary. Not even we can predict if they will eventually join the play. However, we do have a feeling towards people who are not open and we just don't address them. We can see the lack of openness in their body language, when people look away or fold their arms. At a certain point, however, it is impossible even for us to predict how the addressed person will react. In his or her place, I would also naturally react sceptically and hesitantly, and that is the reason why my primary aim as a performer is to build trust.

BT   I think it is fun to make people aware of their boundaries. We know in advance what the spectators have to accomplish and that it is feasible. But it only gets really interesting, when the boundaries remain real. I recall the task called 'Will you kiss a rabbit?' in *Super Night Shot* – we could formulate the task differently, setting the bar higher or lower. What the audience are going to see and what interests us is that someone goes beyond their own limits, that someone will be challenged. That's why we avoid downplaying participation.

JF   Our concern is to thematise the frontier. This is precisely where the utopic moment lies for us all. Participation often makes you feel anxious and you are afraid of looking ridiculous or not living up to your own expectations. We know these frontiers. On the one hand, we don't want to undermine them, but on the other hand, we want to let the other know that we are on equal terms and they cannot do anything wrong.

BT   I believe Gob Squad's pieces convey the feeling that you can come into contact with strangers and achieve something. This is also a social utopia of living together.

JF   We must say, however, that the reaction of the passers-by has strongly changed in the past years. Since people became more suspicious towards the camera in the YouTube era, we have to show more clearly that we don't want to use the camera to turn them into objects.

BT   I also notice signs of wear-out. Before we go to the street in *Super Night Shot*, I worry whether the passers-by are willing to get involved in the play again or if they would rather say no in a culture of mobile phones and selfies, or they explicitly want to know, what happens with the material. One must remember that *Super Night Shot* was developed before YouTube, when people were not so afraid of selfies. Today people are concerned that the things you record may end up on the Internet and stay there available forever. Sometimes I have the feeling that participation in this way is no longer possible.

JF   But we try to make our framing clear and not to overwhelm people. It is like closing a deal, where the other can decide if he wants to join in or not. That makes a big difference and has an influence on how people react. We played *Super Night Shot* in Downtown Los Angeles, where lots of homeless people live, and they are often filmed by television crews without being asked. There it was particularly important to let everyone choose whether the camera should be directed at them or not. Thus I could win the trust of people, who then spoke about homelessness and their problems, because they felt respected.

AC   *Were there cases where you had difficulty in finding someone for a role or even had to give up searching? Do you have a dramaturgical plan B for those cases?*

BT   It is very surprising indeed, how seldom we have to face difficulties. Earlier with *Prater Saga 3*, we had a sophisticated system of plan B and C variants that we rehearsed before each performance but actually never came to use. With *Revolution now!* we had a half-hearted plan B that we never rehearsed, because we assumed based on our experience that the casting would work anyway. It was rather funny when people wanted to take the opportunity to 'complete' the piece from the outside by organising demonstrations or even a flower planting action in front of the theatre independent of us. What is important for us is to make processes transparent. When we have difficulties finding someone for our cause, it means that the audience is interested precisely in this failure.

AC   *Do you have examples for 'bad', undesirable forms of audience participation? Is there something like a bad behaviour or attacks that you don't allow?*

JF   Now and then there are spectators who test the limits, challenging us as performers or who want to burst open the whole system of the *mise-en-scène*. I myself don't find that interesting, because it takes up a lot of time and destroys the framework.

AC   *Does that worry you?*

JF   I think it was a pity, for example, when we were confronted with outside actions for *Revolution Now!,* because they made the flow of the evening quite impossible. We were forced to deal with very dominant people who attracted too much attention. Whereas I find substantial interventions often thrilling.

BT   Yes, in terms of content or subject-matters you can't really make mistakes. The only difficulty we always have is when someone strongly thematises us as a group and starts talking about Gob Squad and our other pieces.

JF   The worst is actually when someone hides himself behind irony and wears a mask. On the other hand, it is also difficult when someone is too open, pours out his or her heart to you and puts too much trust in you. It is a gift, but at the same time I feel responsible for this person and ask myself if they can properly estimate the context in which the things they entrust me with are going to land. I am very concerned about protecting them so that they don't feel disappointed.

AC   *You have discovered a new form of participation unheard of until today on a theatre stage: In* Saving the World *or* Super Night Shot *the actual play takes place in a public place before the theatre performance and is available to the audience only through video broadcast. It is the camera that functions as a witness to the play. But it is far from being a neutral instrument; in fact, it is indispensable in the direct encounters with passers-by. Would you agree?*

BT   We are our own camera man/woman. The passers-by are not followed by an unknown camera, so it is our decision how we will appear, for example how close we go; we define the framework. The camera allows us to draw the boundaries, but it also provides the possibility of intimacy. Since we don't use the camera as a weapon pointed at someone. Most of the time, we are also in the image.

JF   At the same time the camera represents the third party, the audience. If I walked alone on the street, this unique moment would only emerge between me and the other person. It is only through the presence of the camera that a prospective audience can be involved. When making *Super Night Shot* we felt protected by the camera, we were not alone but had the audience around us. We are more courageous when we have the feeling of playing for spectators. But at the same time, paradoxically, we are in fact alone in this situation.

BT   There is a story to it. During the rehearsals we agreed that we should avoid going home with people, as in that case, we would indeed be alone with the camera. A female performer once went to a hotel room with a passer-by, where it became clear that something very different from casting someone who later would kiss a rabbit is supposed to happen. But the security provided by the camera was apparently strong enough to save the performer from this delicate situation. In the end, the man kissed neither the performer nor the rabbit. She felt protected by the prospective audience, even if it wasn't the case in reality.

JF   And the camera always produces an *off* as well. You have the possibility to act outside its framework – you don't necessarily have to go on stage.

189

AC *One of the central questions of this book is how can theatre get involved in social and political issues, perhaps in an even more uncompromising or different manner than on the level of activism and theory. How would you locate the political in your work?*

BT The political could be said to lie in us being replaceable. What is liberating in our way of working might be the changing of roles among each other and also with the audience. There is something unifying in it, something that only a collective can bring about. Our society is longing for heroes, you want to see a genius, to admire it, but this is a bit restrictive, which can lead to serious problems on both sides. To create something in a group, to produce something together, is already a political signal.

JF I would also say that working in a collective is political, namely deliberately political. At the same time you realise that working collectively is quite a challenge to the existing structures of the cultural scene. We realise though, that the more you are divided into different areas of responsibility, as in the case of municipal theatres, the more you lose empathy for each other. It seems quite strange for me when actors have no awareness of what is happening in the other crafts. The political dimension of Gob Squad lies precisely in the fact that the roles are interchangeable, attributions are put in motion, and imperfection is brought into play. The theatre I'm interested in has a utopian potential, because it allows alternative ways of acting and playing.

AC *What exactly is your idea of a utopian theatre?*

JF It consists of crossing boundaries, in the participative tasks, in the interactions with the audience, in coming closer to each other this way. To that purpose we are given a license by art, by the aesthetic framework.

BT The promise of something being created before your own eyes and of your really sitting there is also a utopian gesture of theatre. It also involves the promise of failure, something that is usually avoided in theatre operations. It might be a bit exaggerated, but the reason why people go to the theatre is the hope that something can go wrong. Gob Squad dares to face the possibility of failure in order to accentuate success all the more. When the play comes into being before your own eyes, you can enjoy it in a different way from when the cake comes on stage baked.

JF   There might be something utopian in the great power of micro moments as well, when individuals exceed their own limits. It feels though, that altogether, i.e. in broader social contexts, things could work out differently. Can it be a practice for something bigger?

BT   Yes, participation is often built by Gob Squad in a way that it amounts to a shared moment. With participation it is interesting to let an idea you had or that has arisen in the group touch someone, who is absolutely unprepared. To fight for this moment, to negotiate it, to achieve it together or to let it be taken out of your hands – this is a task which can be incredibly rewarding but also frustrating. In any case it has something utopic about it.

AC   *You often embed micro-utopias of encounters in narratives of grand social utopias, which are unrealisable in the way you act. The casting of the people in* Revolution Now! *torpedoed, for instance, the main principle of revolution. In* Saving the World *there appears the idea of an unlimited inclusion that is unattainable. Why are you intrigued by grand utopias like 'saving humanity' or 'revolution' for instance, and how do you deal with their paradoxes?*

JF   In this context, the tolerance of failure also plays an important role for us. As a matter of fact, we have often envisaged great tasks because we believe that we must think big, we should venture to do and expect great things. You should never give up setting yourself great tasks.

BT   In addition to that, you can eventually define for yourself what success and failure is. In case of a failure, it is not our intention to display helplessness or to communicate: 'We cannot make it anyway!'. We are rather interested in defining success in a different way, finding it in unexpected moments.

JF   I totally agree with that. The sense of fulfilment and failure are hardly separable, they are always open to negotiation for us. As far as utopic themes are concerned, I also see a huge difference to other performance groups working with participation or immersion: for us it is very important to have an 'outside of fiction'. By that I mean the 'before' and the 'after' of the fictionally framed tasks. We try to make the construction of the evening visible.

AC *You are best known for being an independent group, but you also develop pieces in established public theatres. How would you describe your participation in institutional structures and what are the advantages and disadvantages of making a piece in a municipal theatre as was recently the case with* War and Peace *at the Munich Kammerspiele?*

JF I find this question very important, although so far we haven't evaluated the specific experiences from Munich thoroughly enough. Our group comes fundamentally not from the field of theatre but from performance art, which is more closely related to the art world. Hollywood cinema, European arthouse films, pop culture, and pop music are for us much stronger sources of inspiration than the theatre. That is why Gob Squad is in the strange position of still being a fringe act for the mainstream public theatre, representing a challenge for the audience of the Munich Kammerspiele. But at the same time, we are considered in our niche to be somewhat classic, like the mainstream in the niche. This is a schizophrenic position. As for the structural connection, the fact that there are product expectations in municipal theatre causes some friction in the co-operation. But Matthias Lilienthal, the director of the Kammerspiele, is trying to bring the working structures of the municipal theatre and the independent scene closer together, so after the first night, for example, we are even going to have additional rehearsals, which, in fact, poses a challenge to the house. Apart from this, the principle of the interchangeability of roles was, for example, difficult to explain, because not all the members of the ensemble whom we had been working with could perform in the first night. And the fact that there is no cast B for us does not always seem to be comprehensible, neither for the theatre staff, nor for some spectators.

BT In the past we had quite luxurious circumstances, inasmuch as the collective process could take place calmly. But working in a large institution also means that the concerns and hardships of the institution do influence the artistic results. For example, the bilingual nature of Gob Squad has been sacrificed in the past in order to meet the habits of the audience, even if one might have obtained something new from this divergence.

JF   But in Munich we have also advocated strongly for the things that are important to us. Actually, we put up with the fact that we could not expect English proficiency from the audience, because we did not want to talk past each other. We realised only afterwards that giving up bilingualism was not necessarily a good decision. And those are points that we now need to evaluate in order to determine the limits of the compromises we can make.

House on Fire is a network of ten European theatres and festivals that aims to support the production and presentation of politically engaged theatre on an international level. Based on the conviction that the arts have an essential role to play in the development of thought and debate about the challenges that our societies are facing at this turbulent beginning of the century, the partners of House on Fire join forces to pursue an international programming and coproduction policy to support the creation and dissemination of performances that claim a place in the public debate about social, environmental, and political issues.

Besides producing and presenting art works, House on Fire experiments with programming formats that look for new ways to present these works to audiences all over Europe. Taking the theatre into the streets or even into your living room, framing it with debates and conferences, opening it up to audience participation, presenting it in concentrated marathon sessions or spreading it over a year-long thematic focus, stimulating the creation of unexpected forms that combine documentary and fiction, installation and performance, conference and theatre, and activism and art.

Experimentation needs thought. House on Fire dedicates a great deal of attention to the development of discourse around the new forms of political and interventionist theatre that are being created today. The publication series *Performing Urgency* is one of the network's main contributions towards that goal.

Performing Urgency aims at a broader discussion of the conditions, aesthetics, concepts, and topics of contemporary performing arts. Authors include artists, journalists, academic writers from different fields, as well as curators and dramaturgs. Abstract reflections are positioned alongside concrete analyses of artistic work, interviews and statements next to artist pages, as well as concrete proposals for artistic, curatorial, and dramaturgical methodologies.

OPHELIA PATRICIO ARRABAL (CO)
has travelled extensively in Brazil, publishing her travel chronicles in magazines and art catalogues. Her most recent essay, published in *Caderno de Subjetividades*, PUC-SP, examines the potential relationship between art and the street.

ELENA BASTERI (DE/IT)
is an independent curator, writer, and researcher based in Berlin. Her main area of interest lies in the cross field between dance, theatre, and visual art. She holds a MA in Tanzwissenschaft from the Freie Universität in Berlin and she co-edited the book *Rehearsing Collectivity Choreography* (2012).

LOTTE VAN DEN BERG (NL)
uses the theatrical space to make visible how we relate to one another. She does this not only between the walls of the theatre space but also and especially outside of them. Van den Berg is currently working on a long term project entitled *Building Conversation.* This is a dialogical artwork in which she invites participating audiences to join in conversation.

ROGER BERNAT (ES)
uses documents, testimonies, and historical stagings to develop projects in which a community becomes the protagonist. There are no longer individual actors who embody characters but it is the public that, not without irony, represents the community.

JUSTINE BOUTENS (BE)
is head of the communications department at the Ghent based arts centre CAMPO. In the past, she has worked for theatre maker Arne Sierens / Cie. Cecilia and with arts festivals such as Dansand (Vrijstaat O.) and Theater aan Zee (TAZ#12).

ANNA R. BURZYŃSKA (PL)
is a critic, curator, dramaturg, and Assistant Professor at the Department of Theatre at Jagiellonian University in Krakow. She edits the *Didaskalia* theatre journal and has published several books, including *The Classics and the Troublemakers: Theatre Directors from Poland* (2008).

ADAM CZIRAK (DE)

is Assistant Professor in Performance Studies at the Freie University Berlin, Germany. His research focuses on contemporary theatre and performance art in Eastern Europe. His publications include *Partizipation der Blicke* (2012) and *Dramaturgien des Anfangens* (ed. with Gerko Egert, 2016).

JOHANNA FREIBURG (DE)

is co-founder and member of the British-German art collective Gob Squad as well as of the German performance collective She She Pop. Gob Squad have been devising, directing, and performing together since 1994, working where theatre meets art, media, and real life.

HELGARD HAUG, STEFAN KAEGI & DANIEL WETZEL (DE)

are co-founders of Rimini Protokoll. They produce theatre pieces, radio shows, and work in the urban environment in a variety of collaborative partnerships, using research, auditions, and conceptual processes, allowing what they call 'Experts' to find their unique voice. Their works include *Lagos Business Angels* with Nigerian business people (2012), *100% City* with a sample of 100 citizens on stage, as well as *Weltklimakonferenz* (2014), a simulation of the UN Conference on climate change.

TOBI MÜLLER (DE)

is a freelance writer in Berlin. He was an editor at daily newspapers in Zürich and wrote about theatre and pop music. After working for Swiss TV, he moved to Berlin in order to work freelance for print and radio. He has written semi documentary plays, created a film, and curates talks and conferences.

DOMINIQUE NDUHURA (RW)

is a lecturer at the School of Journalism and Communication/University of Rwanda, and now a PhD candidate at Hallym University in South Korea. He has widely researched in the field of media, communication, and Entertainment Education (EE) since 2000. His Master's dissertation was entitled 'Freirean Pedagogy as Applied by DramAidE' (2004).

ANTOINE PICKELS (BE)

works as an artist, writer, curator, teacher, and critic. He currently edits the e-magazine *Klaxon* and curates 'Signal' in Brussels, both dedicated to living art in the public space. His main areas of research are contemporary dance, experimental theatre, live art and performance art, public space living arts, and queer aesthetics.

ADELHEID ROOSEN (NL)

is artistic leader of theatre companies Adelheid Female Economy and Zina. Her immersive and intimate approach, with both professional actors and neighborhood residents, makes her a pioneer in the Dutch theatre scene. She is writer and director of the acclaimed *Veiled Monologues* (2003), *Is.Man* (2006), *UrbanSafari* (2012) & *The Crossing* (2014).

TOM SELLAR (US)

a writer, editor, and curator, is editor-in-chief of Yale's performance journal *Theater* and Professor of Dramaturgy and Dramatic Criticism at Yale University. His criticism and writing have appeared in international publications including *Artforum* and the *New York Times*.

ROBERTO FRATINI SERAFIDE (IT)

is a dramaturg and theoretician in Contemporary Dance. He lectures on Dance Theory for the CSD in Barcelona. He is dramaturg for various international companies (Roger Bernat FFF, Philippe Saire, La Veronal, among others). In 2013 he was awarded the FAD prize. His book *A Contracuento. La danza y las derivas del narrar* was published in 2012.

JAN SOWA (PL)

is dialectical materialist social theorist. He has written several books and dozens of articles encompassing the field of sociology and cultural studies. Sowa has conducted research and lectured at several universities, most recently at the University of São Paulo. He currently remains, by his own choosing, an independent scholar.

BASTIAN TROST (DE)

is one of seven members of the Performance Art Collective Gob Squad. He studied acting at Westfälische Schauspielschule in Bochum and worked as an actor in a number of films (including the first three minutes of the Oscar award winning film *The Lives of Others*) before he joined Gob Squad in 2003. Since then his acting career has declined.

MIRIAM TSCHOLL (DE)

has headed the Bürgerbühne at Dresden's Staatsschauspiel theatre since the 2009-10 season. Her recent work has included *Morgenland* (2015), a production featuring an ensemble of Arabic-speaking Dresden residents. She has also held other directorial roles in Hannover, Berlin, Mannheim, and Freiburg, to name but a few.

TEA TUPAJIĆ (HR)

is a theatre director. As an independent artist she works both in performing and visual arts context. Her projects *The Curators' Piece* (in collaboration with Petra Zanki), *La maladie de la mort*, *Variete Europe*, and *The Disco* are presented internationally.

ANA VUJANOVIĆ (RS/DE)

is an independent cultural worker. She is a member of TkH [Walking Theory], a theoretical-artistic platform. She currently teaches at SNDO Amsterdam and HZT Berlin. Her publications include *TkH journal for performing arts theory* and the book *Public Sphere by Performance* (with B. Cvejić) (2012).

WOJTEK ZIEMILSKI (PL)

is a theatre director and visual artist. He also teaches documentary and devised theatre at the Warsaw University and the National Academy of Dramatic Art in Warsaw. He was one of the authors of the 2014 activist action Golgota Picnic Polska in 30 cities across Poland.